Voices from Syria

Voices from Syria

Mark Taliano

Global Research

Voices from Syria

by Mark Taliano

Global Research Publishers is a division of the Centre for Research on Globalization (CRG), P.O. Box 55019, 11, rue Notre-Dame Ouest, Montréal, Québec, H2Y 4A7, Canada.

For more information, contact the publisher at the above address or by email at our website at www.globalresearch.ca.

FIRST EDITION

Cover Photo © Uchar

Cover graphics by Alex Vlaanderen © Global Research,

Page layout and book design by Réjean Mc Kinnon

Printed and bound in Canada. Printed on chlorine-free 100% post-consumer recycled paper.

ISBN 978-0-9879389-1-6

Library and Archives Canada Cataloguing in Publication

Taliano, Mark, author
  Voices from Syria / Mark Taliano.

ISBN 978-0-9879389-1-6

        1. Syria--History--Civil War, 2011-. 2. Syria--Social conditions.
I. Title.

DS98.6.T34 2017   956.9104'23   C2017-900222-8

This book is dedicated to the people of Syria, all of whom are on the front lines in the fight against international terrorism.

Your blood is being shed for our sins.

Acknowledgements

So many people helped me with this book. Here are but a few.

Thank you to Ken Stone, who inspired me to take the trip to Syria.

Thanks to the organizers of the Third International Tour of Peace to Syria, who made this trip possible, despite barriers, thus giving us the chance to see and hear Syria for our-selves. Now we can better share the truth.

Thanks to my fellow travellers, who are my brothers and sisters in spirit.

Thanks to Professor Michel Chossudovsky who helped me publish this book.

Thanks to Gerry DiSanto at the Defensive Arts Training Centre who encouraged me to write this book.

Last but not least, special thanks to Victoria, who helped me along the way.

About the Author

*Former high school teacher **Mark Taliano** is an author, an independent investigative reporter, and a Research Associate with the Centre for Research on Globalization (Global Research) who recently returned from a trip to Syria with the Third International Tour of Peace to Syria.*

In this book, he combines years of research with on-the-ground observations to present an informed and well-documented analysis that refutes mainstream media narratives about the dirty war on Syria.

— TABLE OF CONTENTS —

FOREWORD

We bring to the attention of our readers Mark Taliano's Book entitled *Voices from Syria.* In contrast to most geopolitical analysts of the Middle East, Mark Taliano focusses on what unites humanity with the people of Syria in their struggle against foreign aggression.

Taliano talks and listens to the people of Syria. He reveals the courage and resilience of a Nation and its people in their day to day

Author: Mark Taliano

lives, after more than five years of US-NATO sponsored terrorism and more than two years of US "peacemaking" airstrikes which have largely targeted Syria's civilian infrastructure.

Everybody in Syria knows that Washington is behind the terrorists, that they are financed by the US (at tax payers expense) and its allies, trained and recruited by America's Middle East partners. Saudi Arabia, Qatar, have been financing and training the ISIS-Daesh, al Nusra terrorists on behalf of the United States. Israel is harboring the terrorists out of the occupied Golan Heights, NATO in liaison with the Turkish high command has since March 2011 been involved in coordinating the recruitment of the jihadist fighters dispatched to Syria.

Moreover, the ISIS-Daesh brigades in both Syria and Iraq are integrated by Western special forces and military advisers.

While all this is known to the Syrian people, Western public opinion is led to believe that the US is leading a "counter-terrorism campaign" in Syria and Iraq against the Islamic State (ISIS-Daesh), an entity created and supported by US intelligence.

"Everything that we saw in Syria speaks of humanity's common heritage", says Mark Taliano. Syria is the cradle of civilization, Mesopotamia, the Land of Two Rivers, where the early civilizations of the fertile crescent took their roots.

Image: Damascus National Museum, M Chossudovsky, 2011

This is what the Washington Neocons want to destroy. But to reach their objective they need to wage a dirty propaganda campaign which conveys the illusion that America is involved in a "humanitarian" "peace-making" undertaking.

The Syrian people know who the real terrorists are. *"The Western assault on this country is an assault on our common humanity, and an assault on Syria's progressive and forward-looking future"*, says Taliano.

Mark Taliano focusses on the truth as an instrument for building peace and counter-propaganda:

> "Should the West's "regime change" operations succeed, the secular, pluralist government of President Assad will be replaced by its opposite: a barbaric, sectarian regime, and chaos.

Yet Western politicians are seemingly propagandized by their own lies. Or perhaps they see no choice but to cravenly follow diktats from above. Humanity's better nature, however, demands that we all open our eyes, that we learn from history, and that we embrace the rule of international law rather than the diktats of a criminal Empire. Syria and Syrians must be saved, not destroyed.

Currently, my interests lie in digging for political truths in a world that is rushing headlong into war and barbarism, on a bedrock of lies.

When I find such truths, their trajectories invariably lead to peace rather than war. So now, my "crusade' is to help share the truth, to make it broad-based, and to make a positive difference.

The dirty war on Syria is such a blatant example of the supremacy of war, deception — and evil — over civilization, and our common humanity, that my current research interests are defined by what does or does not happen there. If Syria wins, we all win. Right now, she is winning."

Mark Taliano refutes the mainstream media. The causes and consequences of the US-led war on Syria, not to mention the extensive war crimes and atrocities committed by the terrorists on behalf the Western military alliance are routinely obfuscated by the media.

Taliano is committed to reversing the tide of media disinformation, by reaching out to Western public opinion on behalf of the Syrian people. *"Syria's stand against the Western agencies of death and destruction is a stand for all of humanity against the dark forces that fester beneath our politicians' empty words and the courtesan media's toxic lies."*

Mark Taliano's **Voices from Syria** provides a carefully documented overview of life in Syria, the day to day struggle of the Syrian people to protect and sustain their national sovereignty.

Prof. Michel Chossudovsky
Director
Centre for Research on Globalization (CRG)

PREFACE

The Syrian Arab Republic (Syria) is an ancient holy land surrounded by terrorist-supporting countries that want to destroy it. These countries, in turn, are supported by the US-led North Atlantic Treaty Organization (NATO).

The secular government of Syria is led by Bashar al-Assad, its elected President. al-Assad is progressive and forward-looking. The terrorists invading and occupying parts of the country are neither progressive nor forward-looking, and most Syrians are happy to be rid of them. Many Syrians are critical of al-Assad for being too soft on the terrorists. They have dubbed him Mr. Soft Heart.

al-Assad has earned the support of most Syrians by providing for them and by protecting them. Healthcare and education, including higher education, are free in Syria. Before the externally orchestrated and perpetrated war on Syria started, Syria was one of the safest countries in the world to visit.

Now that the West has injected terrorists into the country and imposed illegal sanctions on Syrians, the war-torn country and its people are mostly defiant. The future of the country is theirs to decide, as per international law, and they will not be colonized. Their defiance comes easily thanks to the Western-supported, illegal "opposition" that confronts them.

None of the "opposing" terrorists are moderate. They slaughter Christians, minorities, and Muslims alike. They seek a blank slate upon which to impose their extremist Wahhabi ideology, and they seek to erase both Syria's history and its people.

Historical memory teaches us that the West's use of proxy mercenaries is not new. The West has destroyed a series of countries in quick succession since 11 September 2001 (9/11), including but not limited to Afghanistan, Iraq and Libya, all by design, and always aided and abetted by mercenary ground troops.

But Syria has strong institutions and strong allies. It will be victorious, to the benefit of Syrians and humanity.

This book presents the story of Syria and Syrians as they struggle valiantly against NATO terrorism.

The narrative contradicts mainstream messaging, as it must. The West and its agencies could never garner public support for their genocidal campaigns if the truth emerged and was acknowledged by a broad base.

Truth leads to peace, but the governing polities that manipulate us and contaminate the public mindset enrich themselves through war, mass slaughter, and propaganda campaigns. Truth and justice are their unstated enemies.

This book aims to shed light on truth, justice and governing lies, with a view to expanding the reach of global peace and destroying the cancer of terrorism.

We initally recounts the story of Syria as told by Syrians, unfiltered by mainstream media propaganda. We see and hear the trauma lived by defiant, heroic Syrians, and we discover that this ancient, holy land will surely survive the current barbarian invasion to rise again as a beacon of civilization, hope, and dignity.

The externally orchestrated war is being resolved internally – by Syrians, for Syrians – and the solutions are often the fruit of genuine democratic processes, in contrast to the processes masquerading as democracy in the West. Syria insists on being a sovereign nation.

We subsequently elaborates upon the real story of Syria and the drivers behind the current war, in which the US-led Empire is using terrorist proxies to advance its reach, contrary to the wishes of the vast majority of Syrians.

The alternative to Syria's elected government is genocidal despotism and sharia law. The (non-existent) "moderates" cannot be separated from the "extremists" because all of the mercenary terrorists share the same goals and the same ideologies.

The predictable result of engineered deception is that domestic Western populations remain deceived and politically passive. The truth is inverted and large swaths of our populations remain deluded. Whereas the West and its allies support all the terrorists invading Syria, our domestic populations think that we are fighting terrorism. This is the great fraud of the "Global War on Terrorism."

Between 15 and 23 September 2016, I travelled to war-torn Syria because I sensed years ago that the official narratives being fed to North Americans across TV screens, in newsprint and on the internet were false.

The invasions of Afghanistan, Iraq, and Libya were all based on lies; likewise for Ukraine. All of the post-9/11 wars were sold to Western audiences through a sophisticated network of interlocking governing agencies that disseminate propaganda to both domestic and foreign audiences.

But the dirty war on Syria is different. The degree of war propaganda levelled at Syria and contaminating humanity at this moment is likely unprecedented.

I had studied and written about Syria for years, so I was not entirely surprised by what I saw. What I felt was a different story.

Syria is an ancient land with a proud and forward-looking people. To this ancient and holy land we sent mercenaries, hatred, bloodshed and destruction. We sent strange notions of national exceptionalism and wave upon wave of lies.

As a visitor I felt shame, but Syrians welcomed me as one of them. These are their stories; these are their voices.

CHAPTER I
In Their Own Voices

Life in war-torn Syria can be horrific. Most Syrians have been impacted directly by the war and **Ammar** is no exception. This is his story:[1]

> As everyday morning my sister was going to the university when a bloody Takfirist Salafi Wahhabi suicide bomber blew up bomb car at the bus stop which led to the martyrdom and injury of many civilians and university students who were going to their exams. After 10 minutes another suicide bomber blew up himself at the same place, taking advantage of the gathering of people and ambulance teams. Usually when a terror attack happens we call all family members and friends to make sure they all are ok, but this time no one answered! Then we started looking for her in hospitals ... the shock was in the bloody views there; many burned bodies and human body parts were on the ground. There I saw my sister, a body without soul.

Many Syrians have experienced similar losses. **Lilly Martin**, an American living permanently in Syria, writes about why she could not vote for Hillary Clinton:[2]

> She personally oversaw the transfer of weapons from Libya to Turkey to be used specifically by the American-backed terrorists who destroyed my own home on March 21, 2014 and beheaded my Christian neighbors, and raped the old ladies who they kidnapped and took to Turkey, and killed others, and destroyed the whole village of Kessab, Syria. This is not a rumor, this is a fact. This is well documented in her time as Secretary of State.

---

1. Ammar is a pseudonym for an actual Syrian source. He shared his story with me in a private Facebook message dated 1 October 2016. The bombing in Homs occurred on 26 January 2016.
2. Facebook post shared with friends, 12 November 2016.

Martin's testimony about what happened to her in Kessab (Kasab) is corroborated by an eyewitness account from Dr **Declan Hayes**:[3]

Kasab's descent into hell began at 5:30 am precisely on March 21st 2014 when merciless shelling from the Turkish side of the Syrian border rained down on the undefended Armenian village, not only sending its 2,000 residents into panic but portending the apocalypse that was about to befall them. Over 20,000 fanatics from al-Nusra, the Free Syrian Army and a number of other extremist groups swarmed over the border on motor bikes, pick-up trucks and Western ambulances converted into troop and munitions carriers for this blitzkrieg. Though hopelessly outnumbered, lightly armed Syrian troops (the Syrian Arab Army) held off the invaders until the inhabitants could be evacuated. Sunnis, Shias, Alawites and Armenian Christians all fled for their lives from these fanatics, who some Western commentators still insist, against not only all the evidence but against common sense as well, are progressive liberators; several Kasab residents, such as Hovian Khatcherin, found themselves fleeing from these Islamic hordes for the third time, having previously been forced to flee Raqqa and Aleppo for her life. Such are the perils that are part and parcel of daily life for the Levant's remaining Christians and for which there seems to be so little pro-active sympathy beyond Syria's borders.

The "liberators" systematically desecrated all Kasab's churches, they looted the village's graves, they scattered the bones of the deceased around the town for stray dogs to scavenge on, they stripped every house and outhouse of anything of value, window and door frames included, and these fanatical despots even hoodwinked the West's press into praising their actions as some sort of praiseworthy activity against the supposedly tyrannical regime in far-away Damascus.

Kasab's very elderly residents, who were too infirm to flee, were ferried, against their wishes, into Turkey and, like the earlier kidnapped nuns of Ma'lulah, were cynically paraded to pretend their kidnappers had their interests at heart. Pepken

---

3. Dr Declan Hayes. "The Rape of Kasab," Indymedia UK, 3 September 2014. (https://www.indymedia.org.uk/en/regions/world/2014/09/517871.html) Accessed 5 December 2016.

Djourian and his wife find that a particularly bitter pill to swallow as the invaders executed their only son in front of them and let him to rot for three days in the sun before throwing him like a dog into a hastily dug hole in their apple orchard, a particularly apt analogy as his murderer said that Kevork's death meant they "had one less Armenian dog to worry about." Following his murder, Kevork's parents were held against their will for the next forty days in Turkey, where their kidnappers even brought Turkey's American ambassador to admire how well they were being treated and where noted author Nizar Khalil willingly acted as interpreter between the aged Armenian captives and their Turkish captors.

Kasab's residents are convinced all of this was done with the full connivance of the Turkish government. Kasab is in the very north-west tip of Syria and there is no other way to attack it than with the permission of the Turkish authorities through the heavily-militarized hills of nearby Turkey. Indeed, Samuel Poladian, who stayed in Kasab for the entire occupation, lives only 200 metres from a Turkish police station and, like all the others, he not only claims he heard Turkish military helicopters overhead on the morning of the invasion but that Turkey orchestrated the whole outrage. Because the Turkish side of the border is speckled with countless army outposts and because not even one of the invaders nor one of the looters was arrested or even detained on the Turkish side of the border, their claims and their contrary narrative are much more credible than Turkey's lame excuses for these crimes.

The Armenians claim the Kasab outrage, which was directed solely against Armenian Christians, was Turkey's brutal way of showing the Armenians and the Syrian government and army which protect them that, just as in 1909 and in 1915, they can occupy Kasab and slaughter its inhabitants at will any time they choose to. The wilful destruction of the centre of Kasab, together with all its churches, makes sense within that framework. What does not make sense to the people of Kasab, or to those of the Aramaic-speaking town of Ma'lulah I visited a few days earlier, is why they have been so completely and utterly abandoned by the Christians of the West, so much so that the departing fanatics booby-trapped the entire town of Ma'lulah with bombs marked as donations to the Free Syrian Army by the European Union. Neither of these ransacked Christian towns has received even one penny in aid from the West, which seems to focus its relief efforts on the refugee camps the rebel extremists and their Turkish hosts control and use as forward bases to attack those they denigrate and dehumanize as "Cross worshippers" and who we should regard as fellow human beings we are duty bound to help.

Though the Syrian Arab Army retook Kasab on 15 June 2014, the Armenians' nightmare has not ended. Less than 800 of Kasab's more than 2000 residents have returned to their wrecked and looted homes, the schools are bereft not only of all teaching materials, the liberators having burned the lot of it, but also of the wherewithal to replace them with, their orchards, their means of making a living stand fallow, the trees being more "collateral damage" caused by their erstwhile "liberators" who have promised to return again with a vengeance, the Western world, together with the Armenian diaspora, have other "more important" things to concern themselves with, their tormentors commit stomach-churning atrocities on a daily basis and Turkey and other sinister forces lurk in the long grass, waiting to strike at the defenceless Christian Armenians of Kasab whenever is most opportune for their nefarious agendas.

Almost every new story from the West demonizes Vladimir Putin. **Ammar**, however, has direct contact with Russian agencies. This is his assessment:[4]

I see the biggest humanitarian aid provided by our Russian brothers is fighting the US–NATO-founded brutal terrorism and supporting Syrian armed forces (Syrian Arab Army) against Western backed barbarian terrorism, as well standing with Syria in international forums. Furthermore, the Russian aid for in-need Syrian civilians represented in food like rice, sugar, tea, canned meat and fish, and medical aid that includes medicines, emergency medical supplies, antibiotics and medical products for the treatment of a variety of diseases, as well they brought doctors who made physical check up to needy people. These were distributed directly by Russians to needy

4. Shared by Ammar in a private Facebook message to Mark Taliano, dated 1 October 2016.2016.

people. Thanks to American–European sanctions against Syrian people and against Syrian economy, prices got so expensive, economical situation became harder, targeting Syrian infrastructures by the illegal US-led coalition aircrafts, also looting and theft (from) Syrian industrial plants, then sold cheaply to Turkey by their mercenaries. All these reasons increased the suffering of Syrian people.

Martin, for her part, owes her very life to Russian military intervention in Syria. She wrote the following:[5]

Concerning Russia: I rented a summer house in Slounfa, August 15 to September 15, 2015. As you recall, my summer home in Kessab was destroyed, so I rented a summer house in Slounfa, as Kessab was still not safe. I rented there for 30 days. During this time I was on the front battle line of a fierce battle the whole time at Salma. It was scary, and loud, but the mountain cool air was worth the fear. When I left Slounfa, I was convinced that the terrorists would be inside Latakia soon. They had come so close. They were one hour drive away from downtown Latakia. The Syrian Arab Army was so tired, so over-drawn. The TV showed Syrian soldiers very close to my position that reported the fighters they were killing had on Turkish military uniforms and carried Turkish official military ID. When they said that, I knew we weren't fighting plain old terrorists and jihadists, we were actually fighting the Turkish National Army. Turkey is huge compared to Syria. A few days later, I came back home to Latakia and I mentally prepared myself for evacuation. We would flee as soon as the terrorists started to attack the city. They were already shooting missiles at Latakia almost daily, and while I was up there they struck Latakia with eleven missiles in one day, which was the record. It was about ten days later the Russians arrived in full force, and since then the terrorists in our area have been eliminated. I can state Russia saved the Syrian coast. That is correct, and they saved Kessab. However, the big problem is Aleppo. Can we get the US to stop supporting terrorists there? We hope so.

---

5. Shared in a private Facebook message dated 13 November 2016.

The West demonizes the Syrian government and invariably praises the mercenary terrorists, or confuses the narrative to protect the terrorists. This is **Ammar**'s assessment:[6]

>About Syrian government: we support the policy of national reconciliation as we stand with reformation against corruption, and secularism against the criminal Salafi-Takfiri-Wahhabi logic. We hope the government gives more support to Syrian armed forces.
>
>About the Russian assistance, I see it saves the Syrian state and re-balances the world after the USA's domination.
>
>Israel still occupies the Syrian Golan Heights, still gives al-Qaeda terrorists medical treatment and allows them to use occupied lands to fight against Syrian Army (SAA). Many times Israeli air force participated in the fight directly supporting al-Qaeda militants, represented by Jabhat al-Nusra, and bombed Syrian Army (SAA) sites in the south trying to overthrow Syrian state.
>
>US is the mastermind and the main planner of war in Syria. From the first day US took the role of al-Qaeda attorney in Security Council, US intervention and its policy are the main reason of Syrian War. They founded, armed and backed terrorists groups in Syria, and created military training camps for those mercenaries in Jordan and Turkey, and used them in this proxy war. US is supporting al-Qaeda and the other brutal terror groups and recently US gave ISIS (Islamic State of Iraq and Syria) an air cover by targeting Syrian Army (SAA) in Deir Ezzor, which allow ISIS to capture strategic mountain. Also, yes, it seems ISIS has an air force named US Air Force! US lied about Iraq, lied about Libya, and it is lying about Syria. Is bombing Syrian infrastructures (bridges, electricity plants and oil fields) considered fighting terrorism!?
>
>NATO and oil-rich Gulf states are just puppets (…) slaves to their American master. They only implement American orders in collecting, arming, backing, funding mercenaries from all over the world and sending them to fight against Syrians, plus using their media to spread hatred and loathing against minorities. These rotten chiefdoms want to impose sharia law.

6. Shared by Ammar in a private Facebook message to Mark Taliano dated 1 October 2016.

The real story about Syria has been fully documented by Western sources for years. Ammar and Martin's stories bring the truth to the forefront, as they pierce the fog of mainstream media stories, whose sole unstated purpose is to create globalized war, misery and poverty.

The day after the Ghouta attack in September 2013, **Majd al-Zaim** wrote these words:[7]

I am Syrian … living in Syria in the middle of everything. We have seen horrors. It was never a revolution nor a civil war. The terrorists are sent by your government. They are al-Qaeda Jabhat al-Nusra Wahhabi Salafists Talibans etc and the extremist jihadists sent by the West, the Saudis, Qatar and Turkey. Your Obama and whoever is behind him or above him are supporting al-Qaeda and leading a proxy war on my country.

We thought you are against al-Qaeda and now you support them.

The majority here loves Assad. He has never committed a crime against his own people … The chemical attack was staged by the terrorists helped by the USA and the UK, etc. Everyone knows that here.

American soldiers and people should not be supporting barbarian al-Qaeda terrorists who are killing Christians, Muslims in my country and everyone.

Every massacre is committed by them. We were all happy in Syria: we had free school and university education available for everyone, free healthcare, no GMO, no fluoride, no chemtrails, no (…) IMF-controlled bank, (but) state-owned central bank which gives 11% interest, we are self-sufficient and have no foreign debt to any country or bank.

Life before the crisis was so beautiful here. Now it is hard and horrific in some regions. (…)

American people … you gotta regain control of your once admirable country. Now everyone hates you for the death you bring almost everywhere.

Ask the Iraqis … the Afghans … the Pakistanis … the Palestinians … the Syrians … the Macedonians and Serbs …

---

7. Facebook comment by Majd al-Zaim, posted on another's page, 4 September 2013.

> the Libyans ... the Somalis ... the Yemenis ... all the ones you
> kill with drones every day. Stop your wars, Enough wars. Use
> diplomacy ... dialogue ... help ... not force.

Consistent testimonies from Syrians, as well as open-source Western documents and historical memory, all serve to reinforce the accuracy of the aforementioned testimonies.

Syrians are living the horror brought to them by the criminal West. They cannot afford the complacency of shrugging their shoulders in indecision, not when their lives and their ancient civilization is being threatened by Western-paid terrorist mercenaries of the worst kind.

Our proxies slit throats, chop heads, and take no prisoners as we in the West waffle in indecision, ignore empirical evidence, and take the comfortable easy road of believing the labyrinth of lies promulgated by Western media messaging.

The veil of comfortable confusion, nestled in a belief that our government knows best or that it is patriotic to believe the lies and fabrications implicit in the hollow words of politicians (who no longer represent us) and the false pronouncements of imperial messengers, is concealing an overseas holocaust.

Western societies are rotting from the inside out because of these lies and this barbarity. We are protecting a criminal cabal of corporate globalists who do not serve our interests and never will.

Our democracies, which we should be protecting, have long disappeared. Instead we are supporting transnational corporate elites and their delusional projects.

Poverty and disemployment are all soaring beneath the fakery of government pronouncements, as the public domain evaporates beneath words like "efficiency" or the "economy" – all false covers that serve to enrich elites and destroy us. Internal imperialism at home is a faded replica of the foreign imperialism abroad.

As countries are destroyed and its peoples are slaughtered (for example, Syria, Libya, Ukraine, and others) by abhorrent Western proxies, public institutions are contaminated, and ultimately replaced by parasitical privatized facsimiles. Public banking is looted and destroyed in favour of transnational banksterism, World Bank Group funding, and IMF usury. Food security is destroyed and replaced by biotech tentacles and engineered dependencies on cash crops and unhealthy food. Currencies are destroyed, sanctions are imposed, and the unknown, unseen hand of totalitarian control imposes itself amidst the cloud of diversions and confusions, aided by comprador regimes, oligarch interests, and shrugging domestic populations.

Syria refuses to submit. That is why the West is taught to hate it and the rest of the world learns to love and respect it.

Jad Nasr lives in Syria. In September 2016 when I met him in old Damascus, he was 29. He holds a Master's of English Literature and he sometimes uses his considerable talents by serving as translator for Syrian dignitaries, such as the Grand Mufti.

He also has the scar from a bullet wound in his chest and he receives death threats. He explains that terrorists shot him because they did not want to hear the truth. Presumably, the terrorists prefer their own version of the truth, as dictated by Wahhabi-supporting Al Jazeera and Safa TV, as well as all mainstream media messaging promulgated by the West.

Nasr's story is not pleasant. It highlights what Syrians have to endure on a daily basis. He says that his brother was kidnapped last year and that the terrorists tortured him and destroyed his knees. Now he cannot walk. He also told me that his cousin, who was serving in the Syrian Arab Army, lost his leg when Wahhabi suicide bombers attacked his military vehicle. Another cousin was kidnapped in 2012 and remains in captivity.

The terrorists have a talent for kidnapping. Nasr explained that in one operation, they used false flag tactics to capture tanks and ultimately to capture thousands of Syrian soldiers at Douma.

The terrorists also like to showcase their defensive tactics. One of their favourites is to use captives as human shields. Nasr's testimony and video evidence demonstrate kidnapped individuals being put in cages and used as human shields in town squares. Needless to say, when the terrorists occupy towns or parts of towns and cities, they are necessarily using human captives as shields, and the Syrian Arab Army takes tremendous risks by fighting house to house, as they do.

Whereas the United States of America, for example, carpet bombed Fallujah in Iraq, the Syrian Arab Army does not kill Syrian civilians. The terrorists control occupied territories with unspeakable barbarism. **A witness** to the massacre at Adra described the scene in these words:[8]

> The rebels began to attack the government centres, and attacked the police station – where all the policemen were killed after only a brief clash because of the large numbers of attackers. They (the attackers) then headed to the checkpoint located on the edge of the city before moving to the clinic, where they slaughtered one from the medical staff and put his head in the popular market. They then dragged his body in front of townspeople who gathered to see what was happening. Bakery workers who resisted their machinery being taken away were roasted in their own oven. Jabhat al-Nusra and Islamic Front fighters went from house to house with a list of names and none of those taken away then has been seen since.
>
> When the Syrian Army (SAA) would try to enter Adra, the jihadists would throw women and children from the 20,000 people it captured off the top floors in front of the army.

Nasr also discussed the lies propagated by the Western media. He said that for the first three weeks of the so-called "revolution," police and security personnel were ordered to not carry guns. It was during this time that fifteen of Nasr's friends were killed by so-called "peaceful protestors."

This report is corroborated by peace activist **Janice Kortkamp** who writes:[9]

> The media lies about Syria … and I think media heads should face trial for war crimes and crimes against humanity for the one-sided false narrative they've been spreading since the Syrian War began. Even earlier … throughout the entire "Arab Spring," orchestrated by the West using "jihadists" (paid mercenaries, criminals and brain-washed radicals) to create a "New Middle East" dedicated to Western dominance and con-

---

8. Franklin Lamb (with the Syrian Army at Adra al-Omalia) "Massacred Syrian Town Ten Months under Siege Freed by the Syrian Army not the U.S. Coalition." Hwaairfan's Blog. 8 October 2014. (https://hwaairfan.wordpress.com/2014/10/08/massacred-syrian-town-ten-months-under-siege-freed-by-the-syrian-army-not-the-u-s-coalition/) Accessed 5 December 2016.
9. Facebook post shared with friends, dated 11 November 2016.

trol over natural resources.

This soldier, whom we interviewed in Damascus, is a personal hero and friend. A friend to whom I've entrusted my life and would again any time anywhere.

He was one of the soldiers in Daraa in March 2011 (where and when the violence in Syria began). This is his account and it matches several others' first-hand accounts of events there.

The life of a Syrian soldier is so hard. A terrorist paid by the US or Saudi or Qatar makes about $300 or $400 a month. A Syrian soldier receives 1/10th of that. They fight an enemy that is often inhuman. I know of one soldier who was cut to pieces while his terrorist captors had his father on the phone listening to the torturous death of his son.

FALSE: The Syrian War began when President Assad brutally put down peaceful protests.

TRUE: The Syrian War was planned in earnest by the US since 2005. The Syrian soldiers and police were not even allowed to carry weapons until the "peaceful protesters" had slaughtered several hundreds of police and soldiers.

Kortkamp interviewed a **Syrian soldier** who described the soldiers' unarmed and fatal encounters with the initial, externally orchestrated uprisings in these words:[10]

> Soldier: I don't know, we didn't see them face to face. My best friend was shot, so I felt anger and sadness. I felt anger because we were ambushed in this way and all we had was batons, we couldn't defend ourselves. We had to run, they were shooting us like birds. And the demonstrators blocked all the entrances leading to us, so no ambulance was able to reach us whatsoever, at that point. I carried my best friend and what matters for us now is to protect him and protect ourselves until we get to safety. While we were running, we were seeing our friends the civil police, how they were being killed in front of us, or shot at.

Similarly, investigative reporter Rick Sterling debunks the propaganda that "Assad kills his own people" in his description of the

---

10. Gail Malone, "Daily Archives: November 9, 2016." Gailmalone Blog. 9 November 2016. (https://gailmalone.wordpress.com/2016/11/09/) Accessed 5 December 2016.

initial, violent protests:[11] "In reality, there was a violent faction from the start. In the first protests in Deraa, seven police were killed. Two weeks later there was a massacre of 60 security forces in Deraa."

These same "peaceful protestors" were the spearhead of the Western-orchestrated regime-change operations, wherein the Muslim Brotherhood and foreign operatives played central roles. The Arab Spring was a foreign intelligence operation from the beginning.

Recent estimates suggest that terrorists from about 100 countries are currently infesting Syria. This, coupled with the legal interventions of the "Axis of Resistance" and the illegal war crimes of NATO and its allies, means that the war on Syria is increasingly a world war.

Those of us who still believe the lies are enabling imperialists who are pushing us towards the unthinkable.

11. Rick Sterling, "Dissecting the Propaganda on Syria," Consortium News, 6 September 2016. (https://consortiumnews.com/2016/09/06/dissecting-the-propaganda-on-syria) Accessed 5 December 2016.

—————————— CHAPTER II ——————————
The Great Fraud of the Global War on Terrorism

The "Global War on Terrorism," also known as the "War on Terror," is a fraud. It is literally a global war *for* terror. Empire creates and uses extremist terrorist proxies, including ISIS (also called by its Arabic acronym, Daesh), to advance its geopolitical goals.

The Persian Gulf monarchies, Israel, and NATO – including, of course, Turkey – are engaged in a conspiracy to illegally impose regime change on Syria. Failing that, the belligerent nations plan to balkanize the country.

All of these imperial projects are entirely illegal according to Nuremberg standards and all of these projects expand the reach and power of terrorism.

Whereas the West states that it is fighting terrorism, it is in fact creating, aiding and sustaining terrorism. This is the fraud of the operation known as the "Global War on Terrorism."

Imperialism and Syria

The neoconservative "West" and its allies want to destroy the Middle East so that they can control the Middle East.

Under the auspices of their imperial "New Middle East" project, the criminals (US-led NATO, the Gulf Cooperation Council, and Israel), are targeting everything that they falsely profess to cherish.

All of the values that the politicians parade as important, even sacrosanct, are instrumentalized as false fronts that disguise the dark undercurrents dragging humanity towards a barren New World Order of the despair.

Nation–state self-determination, sovereignty, territorial integrity – all vital components of world peace, prosperity and democracy – are, except for their propaganda value, meaningless to elites. A metanational project of top-down control, enforced by these elites, controls how we think, feel and live.

Professor Michel Chossudovsky, author of *America's "War on Terrorism,"* identifies the largely hidden powers behind the system: the global banks and financial institutions, the military–industrial complex, the oil and energy giants, the biotech and pharmaceutical conglomerates, and the powerful media and communications giants, which fabricate the news and influence the course of world events.

This dystopian present has rendered political choices moot. Choices are non-choices, puppet shows sold by empty words and conflicting narratives – all bereft of substance.

The real agenda is unspeakable. The real agenda must be unspeakable because it is poison, a dark distillate of degenerate barbarism, mostly hidden from view.

This real agenda, masked beneath the propaganda technique of the Big Lie and the stories told by scripted politicians, imposes its dark will. There are no mistakes. It is all by design.

War planners knew full well that the sanctions imposed prior to the invasion of Iraq were targeting children. They accurately predicted when the water infrastructure would fail and how many lives would be lost.

A Defense Intelligence Agency document[12] dated 22 January 1991 accurately predicted that, "It probably will take at least six months (to June 1991) before the (water treatment) system is fully degraded," and that "failing to secure supplies will result in a shortage of pure drinking water for much of the population. This could lead to increased incidences, if not epidemics, of disease."

The end result? Over 500,000 children under the age of five were killed with intent (murdered), in addition to over one million other people, none of whom had committed a crime.

The West regularly targets innocent people, including children, with a view to weakening the morale of countries about to be conquered. Madeleine Albright infamously intoned that the "price (murdering 500,000 children) … is worth it," in one of the rare moments when dark truths and media messaging intersect.

---

12. "Iraq Water Treatment Vulnerabilities," filename 511rept.91, dated 22 January 1991 and partially declassified in 1995, can be found on the Pentagon's web site (www.gulflink.osd.mil/declassdocs/dia/19950901/950901_511rept_91.html) Accessed 5 December 2016.

Wilful Destruction of Iraq's Water Supply due to Sanctions

Excerpt from "Iraq Water Treatment Vulnerabilities," 22 January 1991.

FM: DIA WASHINGTON DC

TO: CENTCOM

INFO: CENTAF, UK STRIKE COMMAND, MARCENT,

18 ABC, NAVCENT, SOCCENT, 7TH CORPS, ANKARA

SUBJECT: IRAQ WATER TREATMMENT VULNERABILITIES (U) AS OF 18 JAN 91 KEY JUDGMENTS.

1. IRAQ DEPENDS ON IMPORTING-SPECIALIZED EQUIPMENT-AND SOME CHEMICALS TO PURIFY ITS WATER SUPPLY, MOST OF WHICH IS HEAVILY MINERALIZED AND FREQUENTLY BRACKISH TO SALINE.

2. WITH NO DOMESTIC SOURCES OF BOTH WATER TREATMENT REPLACEMENT PARTS AND SOME ESSENTIAL CHEMICALS, IRAO WILL CONTINUE ATTEMPTS TO CIRCUMVENT UNITED NATIONS SANCTIONS TO IMPORT THESE VITAL COMMODITIES.

3. FAILING TO SECURE SUPPLIES WILL RESULT IN A SHORTAGE OF PURE DRINKING WATER FOR MUCH OF THE POPULATION. THIS COULD LEAD TO INCREASED INCIDENCES, IF NOT EPIDEMICS, OF DISEASE ...

28. THE ENTIRE IRAQI WATER TREATMENT SYSTEM WILL NOT COLLAPSE PRECIPITOUSLY, ... FULL DEGRADATION OF THE WATER TREATMENT SYSTEM PROBABLY WILL TAKE AT LEAST ANOTHER 6 MONTHS.

The unilateral, criminal sanctions against Syria and Syrians are exacting a terrible toll. Dr Justine Walker writes in "National Agenda for the Future of Syria" that "The combined effect of comprehensive, unilateral sanctions, terrorist concerns and the ongoing security environment have created immense hurdles for those engaged in delivering immediate humanitarian aid and wider stabilization pro-grammes."[13]

SUBJECT: (S//NF) [(b)(3): 10 USC § 424] FORMER-LIBYA MILITARY WEAPONS
Shipped to Syria via the Port of Benghazi, Libya

DATE OF INFORMATION: (U) 1 May 2012 - 1 Sep 2012.

CUTOFF: (U) 18 Sep 2012.

[(b)(3): 10 USC § 424,(b)(3); 50 USC § 3024(i)]

WARNING: (U) THIS IS AN INFORMATION REPORT, NOT FINALLY EVALUATED
INTELLIGENCE. REPORT CLASSIFIED SECRET//NOFORN.

TEXT: 1. (S//NF) EXECUTIVE SUMMARY. Weapons from the former Libya
military stockpiles were shipped from the port of Benghazi, Libya to

14-L-0!

[(b)(3): 10 USC § 424]

the Port of Banias and the Port of Borj Islam, Syria. The weapons
shipped during late-August 2012 were Sniper rifles, RPG's, and 125mm
and 155mm howitzers missiles.

2. (S//NF) During the immediate aftermath of, and following the
uncertainty caused by, the downfall of the ((Qaddafi)) regime in
October 2011 and up until early September of 2012, weapons from the
former Libya military stockpiles located in Benghazi, Libya were
shipped from the port of Benghazi, Libya to the ports of Banias and
the Port of Borj Islam, Syria. The Syrian ports were chosen due to
the small amount of cargo traffic transiting these two ports. The
ships used to transport the weapons were medium-sized and able to
hold 10 or less shipping containers of cargo. (NFI)

3. (S//NF) The weapons shipped from Libya to Syria during late-August
2012 were Sniper rifles, RPG's, and 125mm and 155mm howitzers
missiles. The numbers for each weapon were estimated to be: 500
Sniper rifles, 100 RPG launchers with 300 total rounds, and
approximately 400 howitzers missiles [200 ea - 125mm and 200ea - 155
mm].

---

13. Dr Justine Walker. "National Agenda for the Future of Syria: Humanitarian Impact of Syria-Related Unilateral Restrictive Measures" Office of the United Nations
Resident Coordinator in the Syrian Arab Republic. Published by Swiss Agency for
Development and Cooperation SDC, page 6. The Intercept 28 September 2016
(https://theintercept.com/document/2016/09/28/humanitarian-impact-of-syria-re-
lated-unilateral-restrictive-measures/) Accessed 11 December 2016.

War planners also knew that they were supporting al-Qaeda ground troops in Libya when they exploited the Responsibility to Protect (R2P) clause to bomb the sovereign state of Libya, to assassinate Muammar Gaddafi, to destroy water infrastructure, to loot, to plunder, to commit genocide, and to set up an ISIS stronghold. Prior to the invasion, Libya's standard of living was the highest in Africa. There were no mistakes.

The weapons ratline from Libya to Syria was not a mistake either. The West intentionally funded its terrorist proxies so that they would be well provisioned to invade Syria. The weaponization and training of its terrorist foot soldiers supplement the terrorists' now dwindling additional sources of income, such as funding from illicit drugs, the plunder of historical Syrian artifacts, the theft of Syrian oil resources, and so on, all planned by the West. Again, no mistakes.

Defense Intelligence Agency document 14-L-0552/DIA, pages 1–3, dated May through the end of August 2012 and released in April 2015, clearly reveals that, in the aftermath of the West's destruction of Libya, the Libyan armouries were looted and the weapons sent to Syria.

The report confirmed that:[14]

Western intelligence agencies, allied with Wahhabi Saudi Arabia and Pakistan's Inter-Services Intelligence (ISI), perpetuate the degeneracy by raising new recruits into the culture of the un-Islamic Wahhabi ideology. Ahmed Rashid explains that:[15]

> In 1979, 'the largest covert operation in the history of the CIA (Central Intelligence Agency)' was launched in response to the Soviet invasion of Afghanistan.
>
> With the active encouragement of the CIA and Pakistan's ISI (Inter-Services Intelligence), who wanted to turn the

---

14. Defense Intelligence Agency document 14-L-0552/DIA/1-3; dated October 2012 and containing information from 1 May 2012 to 1 September 2012, released 10 April 2015. The three pages can be found on Judicial Watch. (https://www.judicial-watch.org/wp-content/uploads/2015/05/Pgs.-1-3-2-3-from-JW-v-DOD-and-State-15-812-DOD-Release-2015-04-10-final-version1.pdf) Accessed 10 December 2016.

15. Ahmed Rashid, "The Taliban: Exporting Extremism" Foreign Affairs, November-December 1999. Quoted by Michel Chossudovsky in America's War on Terrorism. Hushion House; 2nd revised edition. 1 January 2005.

Afghan jihad into a global war waged by all Muslim states
against the Soviet Union, some 35,000 Muslim radicals from
forty Islamic countries joined Afghanistan's fight between
1982 and 1992. Tens of thousands more came to study in Pak-
istani madrasahs. Eventually, more than 100,000 foreign Muslim radicals were directly influenced by the Afghan jihad.

Just as the CIA, through the ISI, creates "radicals" by indoctrinating
children in "madrasah" schools, so too ISIS indoctrinates Syrian children in the ways of Wahhabi ideology in ISIS-occupied areas of Syria.

In "U.K: Jihadists as 'Charity Workers',"[16] Samuel Westrop writes
that ISIS has supplemented its violence with da'wah programs – a
system of social provision, or "soft-power outreach" – in areas under
its control. A key component of this particular da'wah (normally just
defined as the proselytizing of Islam) is providing educational outreach initiatives "as part of its wider strategy to foster a new gener-
ation of Syrians in support of its ideological agenda."

This un-Islamic ideology is intentionally promoted in occupied
areas of secular, pluralist, democratic Syria with a view to
"weaponizing" children and destroying the country with a cancer of
Wahhabism and violence.

None of this is accidental. All of it is the fruit of considerable fore-
thought and planning by the imperial West, its allies, and their intelligence agencies. Whereas the West proclaims that it is spreading
democracy, it is spreading terrorism, Wahhabism, death and destruction in each of its pre-planned imperial invasions.

Syria's stand against the Western agencies of death and destruction is a stand for all of humanity against the dark forces that fester
beneath our politician's empty words and the media's toxic lies.

International Capital and Syria

Predatory capitalism is a hidden driver beneath Western barbarism, and Syria is on the front lines against the dictatorship of this

---

16. Samuel Westrop, "UK: Jihadists as 'Charity Workers'," Gatestone Institute, 10
April 2014. (www.gatestoneinstitute.org/4258/uk-jihadists-charity-workers) Accessed 5 December 2016.

globalizing economic ideology that favours the dominance of capital and markets over people and nation–states.

Wahhabi Saudi Arabia, the Gulf monarchies, Israel, and NATO are trying to impose this hidden driver of imperialism, called "International Capital," on Syria.

Robin Mathews describes our capture by international capital in "The Trans Pacific Partnership: Canada and Imperial Globalization":[17]

> A characteristic of Imperial Globalization is criminal manipulation of people and events for the profit of a few. It includes massive 'disinformation' about equality, benefits, social development, law, improved standards of living, etc. The disinformation is spread by 'authoritative' news sources. In the hands of gigantic, wealthy, private corporations, globalization is a process which works to erase sovereign democracies and replaces them with 'treated' sub-states, economic colonies ruled by faceless, offshore, often secret, unaccountable powers.

Whereas Canadians are led to believe that we live in a free and democratic society, we are increasingly engineered to accept the dictatorship of transnational capital as expressed through international banking institutions (as opposed to publicly owned banks) and "free trade" agreements, all of which subordinate elected polities and serve the interests of an international oligarch class, to the detriment of Canadians. Both domestically and internationally, wealth is increasingly concentrated in the hands of the few.

So how did Syria, free from terrorists prior to the pre-planned, "interventions," earn the distinction of being on the front lines against the West?

Syria insists on choosing its own path and refuses to be a vassal of US-led forces of predatory capitalism that siphons the world's resources for the benefit of a transnational oligarch class.

---

17. Robin Matthews, "The Trans Pacific Partnership: Canada and Imperial Globalization - Part one," American Herald Tribune. 20 May 2016.
(http://ahtribune.com/world/americas/916-ttp-canada.html). Accessed 26 November 2016.

Imperialists, on the other hand, view international law as a disposable commodity.

Countries are opened up for the extraction of human and natural resources. Transnational banksters pry open previously sovereign countries with usurious loans and bundled structural adjustment programs that privatize and loot public assets for the benefit of the publicly bailed-out "private" Market.

When all else fails, when sanctions have not killed and demoralized enough innocent civilians – the "other" – non-compliant civilized nations – face the Empire's foot soldiers – the likes of which include ISIS–Daesh and al-Qaeda/Al-Nusra Front in Syria.

Zafar Bangath, director of the Institute of Contemporary Islamic Thought and President of the Islamic Society of York Region, Toronto, explained during an interview in June 2016 that Empire is seeking to install a compliant puppet government in Syria, destroy Syria, and protect Israeli supremacy. Already, he notes, the aggressors have inflicted about $100 billion worth of damage on the battered country.

Bangath's assessment errs on the side of caution. A study by *The Lancet* titled "Syria: end sanctions and find a political solution to peace"[18] indicates that by the end of 2014, the cost of illegal sanctions imposed on Syria stood at US $143.8 billion and that 80 per cent of the population was living in poverty.

President al-Assad is well aware of the imperial forces behind the mercenaries invading his country. In a speech to the newly elected members of the People's Assembly of Syria (Syria's Parliament) on 6 June 2016, he elaborated upon the *modus operandi* of the invaders:[19]

• They seek to attack the constitution by means of a so-called "transition" stage

---

18. Waleed Al-Faisal, Kasturi Sen, and Yasser Al Saleh. "Syria: end sanctions and find a political solution to peace." The Lancet, Published 27 May 2015 and in Vol. 3, No. 7, July 2015. (DOI: http://dx.doi.org/10.1016/S2214-109X(15)00046-7)
19. "President al-Assad: Our war on terrorism continues, we will liberate every inch of Syria," Syrian Arab News Agency, 7 June 2016. (http://sana.sy/en/?p=79525) Accessed 5 December 2016.

- They seek to destroy the two pillars of the government: the army and the diverse, national, pan-Arab and religious identity of Syrians
- They seek to rebrand the savage terrorists as "moderates" and then to eternally provide them with a cover of legitimacy
- They seek to create chaos, sectarianism, and ethnic enclaves that turn the people's commitment from the homeland to conflicting groups that seek help from foreigners against their own people
- They seek to be branded as "humanitarian" and "protectors" to save the people from (externally engineered) conflict and misery.

By imposing economic and armed terrorism on the people, by waging a phony war against their own proxies, and by destroying a country's infrastructure, the imperialists seek to be seen as saviours, humanitarians and protectors, who can then introduce the "free market" of international capital, which will be the *coup de grâce* to effect the final destruction of the host country.

We have seen the same script play out most recently in Libya and Iraq.

In "Aspiring to Rule the World: US Capital and the Battle for Syria," Stephen Gowans explains:[20]

Significantly, every country in which the United States has intervened militarily either directly or through proxies, or threatened militarily, since WWII has had a largely publicly owned economy in which the state has played a decisive role, or has had a democratized economy where productive assets have been redistributed from private (usually foreign) investors to workers and farmers, and in which room for US banks, US corporations and US investors to exploit the countries' land, labor, markets and resources has been limited, if not altogether prohibited. These include the Soviet Union and

20. Stephen Gowans. "Aspiring to Rule the World: US Capital and the Battle for Syria." What's Left. 28 November 2015. (https://gowans.wordpress.com/2015/11/28/aspiring-to-rule-the-world-us-capital-and-the-battle-for-syria/) Accessed 5 December 2016.

its allied socialist countries: China, North Korea, Nicaragua, Yugoslavia, Iraq, Libya, Iran, and now Syria. We might expect that a foreign policy dominated by a wealthy investor class would have this character.

Professor John McMurtry further explains that the target nation invariably has more advanced social structures than its neighbours, and that this contradicts the West's agenda which seeks supranational corporate control of resources and markets. The agenda, then, is to destroy these societal structures with a view to replacing them with parasitical models that enrich the oligarch classes and impoverish the masses. It is a globalized settler/colonial dynamic, where the masses, including those in the NATO aggressor nations, are impoverished and lose their "social life bases" as the domestic and international oligarch classes enrich themselves. Consider the examples of Iraq, Libya, Syria.

In "Living Conditions In Iraq: A Criminal Tragedy, " Ghali Hassan reports that, prior to 1991, Iraq had one of the best health care systems in the Middle East and one of the best education systems, as well as modern sanitary and water infrastructure systems. He reports that Iraq ranked fifty out of 130 in the United Nations Development Program's Human Development Index.

Hassan further wri tes that prior to the NATO invasion, Libya had the highest standard of living in Africa, a high Human Development Index ranked above the regional average, free public healthcare, free public education, an 89 per cent adult literacy rate (with girls outnumbering boys by 10 per cent in secondary and tertiary education), subsidized affordable food, and almost no homelessness.

A similar narrative emerges with Syria. In an article by Eva Bartlett, Dr Shaabban, a former professor at Eastern Michigan University and now Political and Media Advisor to President al-Assad, recounts that:[21]

Syria was formerly one of the fastest developing countries in the world, and one of the safest. We have free education and

21. Eva Bartlett, "The Real Syrian Moderates: Voices of Reason," Russia Today, 15 March 2015. (https://www.rt.com/op-edge/240797-syria-moderate-voices-peace-stability/) Accessed 5 December 2016.

health care. We did not know poverty; we grew our food and produced our own clothing. At universities, 55 percent of the students were women.

Syria, then, is opposing international forces of capital that threaten its very existence. These imperial forces are trying to impose a globalized dictatorship of capital that expresses itself externally in the economic sanctions and the invading terrorists ravaging Syria, even as it expresses itself through "internal imperialism" in Western countries such as Canada, where public resources are increasingly looted for the benefit of international investors and oligarch classes, foreign and domestic.

Instead of worshipping at the altar of transnational predatory capitalism, which is spreading war and poverty throughout the world, we should be embracing "Life Capital" and the forces of economic and political democracy that accompany it.

CHAPTER III
Feigned Humanitarianism as Cover for Crimes of the Highest Order

P art of the apparatus of deception involves feigning humanitarianism but delivering the opposite. Canada, for example, is currently branding itself in terms of humanitarianism, and the concrete gesture of accepting Syrian refugees – of which families, women, children, and gay men and gay women are prioritized – is laudable, and no doubt a godsend to those seeking refuge from the foreign mercenary terrorists who are invading Syria.

But the photo-ops also serve to obfuscate the correct diagnosis and cure for the disease afflicting Syria.

When Canada sells military equipment to Saudi Arabia, Canada is part of the disease. More importantly, Canada contributes to the cause of the disease metastasizing overseas when it chooses to ally

Syrian parliamentary elections, 2016 (SANA)

itself with the cancer rather than the cure. The cancer is NATO and its allies, including Saudi Arabia, Qatar, and Jordan. We are the countries funding the terrorists, and we are the cancer that wants to illegally impose regime change in Syria. Canada's Minister of National Defence, Harjit Sajjan – amidst unproven allegations about President al-Assad's "brutality" – asserted that "President Assad, he does need to go, given the complexity of the problem and the horrible atrocities that have been committed to his own people."[22] Sajjan's words demonizing President Assad were totally detached from reality.

On April 18, 2016, Canadian peace activist Ken Stone filed a report from Damascus, in which he described the hotly contested parliamentary elections. He reported that "Tuesday's Syrian election was a vote of confidence by the Syrian people in their government. 5,085,444 voters cast their ballots out of a possible 8,834,994 eligible voters."[23]

Syrians citizens waving national flags and holding photos of Syrian President Bashar Assad during a pro-government rally in Aleppo province, Syria, April 29, 2014 (SANA)

22. "Defence Minister Sajjan on Syria: Assad must go." CTV News. 22 November 2015. http://www.ctvnews.ca/politics/defence-minister-sajjan-on-syria-assad-must-go-1.2669381
23. Ken Stone, "Live from Damascus: The Syrian Election Results," Global Research. 18 April 2016. (http://www.globalresearch.ca/live-from-damascus-the-syrian-election-results/5520592) Accessed 5 December 2016.

Despite the dislocations of war and the threat of terrorism, the participation rate of eligible voters was 58 per cent, the same as Canada's most recent federal elections – and the National Unity Coalition, consisting of the ruling Ba'ath Party and its allies, won 200 of the 250 seats at the People's Assembly.

Even more impressive were the 2014 Presidential election results. Whereas terrorist-occupied areas did not have elections, as was the case with the more recent parliamentary elections described by Stone, the government-secured areas had a voter turnout of 73.4 per cent, and 88.7 per cent of those voted for President al-Assad.[24]

"Brutal dictators" who "bomb their own people" do not garner this type of support from their populations.

Nonetheless, Sajjan's position indicates that Canada supports the U.S strategy – as outlined by Defense Intelligence Agency document 14-L-0552/DIA/287-293 – to use criminal terrorists, most recently branded as ISIS, to destroy the sovereign country of Syria and topple its legal government. Canada, in association with NATO and its allies, wants to make Syria safe for terrorists, and some form of theocracy, consistent with the ongoing NATO strategy of using fanatical terrorists to destroy Iraq, Libya, and Ukraine. Iraq is still infested with Western-allied terrorists – where there were none before the illegal invasion of Iraq in 2003.

Libya is now infested with terrorists – the same ones supported by NATO during its illegal regime-change operation; and Ukraine is infested with neo-Nazi associated terrorists, elements of which were suppressed prior to NATO's meddling. Unlike Western "interventions" in Syria, Russia's intervention conforms to the rule of international law: President al-Assad invited Russia's military assistance into Syria, and the UN Security Council approved it. So, while Russia is making Syria safe for Syrians, the West is doing the opposite. Russia's military assistance, if successful, will cure the terror disease in Syria and therefore solve the refugee problem by making Syria safe for everyone, including families, women, children and homosexuals. If the direct causes of terrorism are not identified and addressed, the flood of refugees will continue and more countries will be impacted by Terror Inc. On the one hand, NATO countries are enabling and supporting terrorism, while on the other they are saving face and hiding their criminality by accepting refugees. From a public relations point of view, it works. But if NATO's intentions were humanitarian, it would stop supporting the terrorists.

It should not be complicated. There would not be refugees if the disease was correctly diagnosed and treated. Part of a correct diagnosis would not only include recognition of our criminal complicity in the destruction of Syria, but also a recognition of Syria's attributes and al-Assad's contributions to the country. An article ironically titled "Les crimes de Bashar al-Assad depuis juin 2000 ("The Crimes of Bashar al-Assad since June 2000")" lists some of al-Assad's notable accomplishments:[25]

- Construction and restoration of 10,000 mosques and 500 churches.
- Construction and restoration of 8,000 schools, 2,000 institutes and 40 universities.
- Construction of more than 600,000 apartments/houses for young people.
- Construction and modernization of more than 6,000 hospitals and clinics.
- Establishment of five international industrial areas.
- Opening of 60 international banks in Syria.
- Opening of Syria to 5 telecommunications operators (Internet service providers and GSM).
- Licenses for 20 independent newspapers and magazines and 5 satellite TV stations.
- Development of performance art, theatre, comedy, tragedy. More than 20,000 Syrian actors achieved Excellence Award.
- Construction and modernization of stadiums and sports arenas. Large global reputation of Syrian athletes in horseback riding, swimming, wrestling, gymnastics and others ...
- Nominal salary increases of 300%.
- Development and modernization of the Syrian Arab Army.
- The economic situation in Syria is healthy, all while the economic crisis affected the world.

---

25. "Les crimes de Bachar al-Assad depuis juin 2000," Réseau International. 25 August 2015. (http://reseauinternational.net/les-crimes-de-bachar-al-assad-depuis-juin-2000/) Accessed 5 December 2015. Translation.

- Thousands of new businesses: restaurants, hotels, tourist sites, leisure centres, shopping centres, factories …
- The fall in unemployment from 28% to 12%, despite the rise in the number of people entering the labour market.
- Connections: electricity, telephone, drinking water and sanitation to more than a million houses and apartments across the country.
- Reimbursement of all debts of the country and 600% increase in agricultural and industrial capacity.
- Development of tourism. Syria was the 3rd most visited Arab country and the 83rd most visited country in the world.
- Syria has only a 1% illiteracy rate; the best score in Asia and Africa.
- Development of public transportation, airports, ports and bus stations, and prices are kept low.
- Constitution of thousands of associations for the poor, orphans and the disabled.
- Syria is the most important country in the region, economically, politically, militarily … and al-Assad is the most influential personality.

al-Assad's reforms recall those of the Gaddafi government before Libya was destroyed by NATO and its allies.

Professor Tim Anderson explains that the Western terrorists have consistently attacked Syria's hospitals and that, between 2011 and 2013, they attacked sixty-seven of the country's ninety-four national hospitals.

Starvation is another strategy used by colonizers to destroy and subjugate populations. Miri Wood explains in "Syria Dying, UN Cyclops Lying. Still"[26] that:

> These *degenerates* are blatantly lying, blaming hunger in Syria that did not exist 5 years ago, on the Syrian government. The P3 of the UN Mafioso clique "ambassadors" (US, UK, France, a.k.a. 'F*UK*US') appear to be playing a ball game, *volleying* 'siege and starvation,' 'starve or surrender' back and forth …

---

26. Miri Wood "Syrians Dying, UN Cyclopes Lying. Still." Syria News. 15 January 2016. (http://www.syrianews.cc/syrians-dying-un-cyclopes-lying-still/) Accessed 5 December 2016.

Wood noted in an earlier piece that Western terrorists steal and horde food supplies with a view to inducing starvation and subjugating populations. Starved populations tend to be more compliant to an occupier's demands when the occupier controls the food.

Lilly Martin corroborates this reality:[27]

> My friend spoke by cell phone to her immediate relatives who are still held hostage inside East Aleppo. They have no food. Desperate to get out. As their houses are smashed, they simply move to a house which is in liveable shape. They are trying to get out. They begged the Free Syrian Army to allow them to leave, the FSA said no. They waved a white flag from their window, thinking if the Syria Arab Army arrived, they could get evacuated, the FSA shot at them and told them to get rid of the white flag. They know that many people are getting out, from phone calls with others, who have said they got out and are checking on their status. They lost six members of the family a few days ago. That family was fleeing a village called Bab not far from Aleppo. There was a checkpoint run by ISIS and they shot the whole family. Witnesses called others and reported it to the family. The bodies were taken to Turkey. The family member who are in East Aleppo have said, as of today, their plan is to get up at first light tomorrow morning, and get with a large group of civilians and all make a dash for the exit. They have been watching the Syrian Arab Army advancing so rapidly, like clockwork. The terrorists are retreating, and will either surrender, or be killed soon. It appears, from the eye witness testimony by cell phone this morning, that the Syrian Arab Army might be in the position tomorrow or the next day to declare the area clean and free of terrorists. Now to feed and find shelter for all these poor people who have been held hostage for over three years, by the American–European supported terrorists, not to mention Australian and Gulf monarchies. Every house will be rebuilt in Syria and USA and her EU and Arab allies will pay for every nail.

Martin's story is corroborated by a 9 September 2016 statement from the UN Commissioner of Human Rights, who accuses the Abu

---

27. Facebook post shared with friends dated 28 November 2016, 1:27 p.m.

Amara battalion and Jabhat Fatah al-Sham (formerly al-Nusra Front/al-Qaeda in Syria) of using civilians as pawns and preventing them from leaving.[28]

Analyst and commentator Sarah Abdallah further elaborates upon the terrorists' use of coercive techniques:[29]

> Syrian Arab Army's remarkable East Aleppo advancement continues:
>> Four more districts freed today, including the pivotal region of Sakhour. In the last 48 hours alone, 12 East Aleppo districts have been liberated. From one area to

Laith Yusef, a member of "Jabhat al-Nusra" terrorists, on top of the destroyed construction of Naba'a Barada (the Barada spring) near the town of E'yn-El-vijeh west of Damascus, happily raising his fingers with "V" sign after blowing-down the only drinking-water supply source for about 6 million people living in Damascus... (Photo: Facebook)

---

28. Rupert Colville (UN High Commissioner for Human Rights spokesperson), "Switzerland: UN says militants blocking civilians from leaving E. Aleppo" Ruptly TV. 9 December 2016. (https://www.youtube.com/watch?v=ZPgTxC04vdM) Accessed 10 December 2016.

29. Vanessa Beeley. "Aleppo Updates: Tears, Hugs and Smiles, the Relief of Escaping Imprisonment in East Aleppo," 21st Century Wire. 29 November 2016. (http://21stcenturywire.com/2016/11/29/aleppo-updates-tears-hugs-and-smiles-the-relief-of-escaping-imprisonment-in-east-aleppo/) Accessed 5 December 2016.

the next, the "moderate" terrorists are melting down. Most important news today though is the SAA's recapture of the Suleiman al-Halabi Water Pumping Station. The Aleppo water crisis is over! Since 2012, Turkish-backed "jihadists" have withheld water from Aleppo's residents as a means of blackmailing them into supporting the "revolution". This has led to unprecedented levels of sickness and malnourishment. But now, the SAA has restored water to more than one million people as it moves ever-closer to freeing Aleppo entirely.

After the liberation of Aleppo in December, 2016, terrorists destroyed and poisoned water sources and infrastructure that serve Damascus. Additionally, SANA news reported on December 30, 2016, that terrorists cut off water supplies to Aleppo.

As with the sanctions on Iraq, wilfully depriving citizens of water contravenes the Geneva Conventions. Article 54 of a 1979 protocol relating to "the protection of victims of international and armed conflicts states:"[30]

It is prohibited to attack, destroy, remove, or render useless objects indispensable to the survival of the civilian population, such as foodstuffs, agricultural areas for the production of foodstuffs, crops, livestock, drinking water installations and supplies and irrigation works, for the specific purpose of denying them for their sustenance value to the civilian population or to the adverse Party, whatever the motive, whether in order to starve out civilians, to cause them to move away, or for any other motive.

The West's illegal sanctions are also part of the siege on Syria and its peoples. Twenty-three million Syrians are daily besieged by these sanctions. Syrian Hospital Director, Dr Munir Rothman reports:[31]

---

30. Customary IHL (International Humanitarian Law) Database. "Practice Relating to Rule 54. Attacks against Objects Indispensable to the Survival of the Civilian Population," International Committee of the Red Cross (ICRC). (https://ihl-databases.icrc.org/customary-ihl/eng/docs/v2_rul_rule54) Accessed 5 December 2016.
31. U.S. Peace Council sharing Vanessa Beeley's global Facebook post on 23 November 2016.
(https://www.facebook.com/USPeaceCouncil/posts/1724197011235104) Accessed 10 December 2016.

We have seen the photos of Omran. It is sad, but there are many more Omrans. We have seen the maggots under the skin of injured children simply because of a lack of basic medical supplies. Children are dying from simple milk shortages in certain areas ... It is our belief in our country and people that enables us to keep working through this crisis.

He adds that:

MSF (Doctors without Borders) supply nothing at all for government hospitals. I have colleagues in Europe who tried to raise funds for our hospital. They are not allowed to do so, yet doctors who support the so-called "rebels" have no such restrictions imposed upon them.

This adds to the accumulation of evidence that Western non-governmental organizations are in fact not impartial, and that they serve the needs of the terrorists and not those of the rest of the population. Investigative reporter Vanessa Beeley adds:[32]

Thanks to the US/EU sanctions it is becoming almost impossible to replace equipment. Research facilities have stopped altogether. Banks in France that worked with the hospital (University Hospital, Latakia) prior to 2011 will be sanctioned by the US if any medical equipment is allowed into Syria from France.

Indiscriminate bombing of civilian populations also serves to subjugate, and create internal and external refugees – another Western specialty. During the occupation of East Aleppo, terrorists fired mortars and assorted bombs into civilian areas daily.

All of this is happening behind a curtain of lies – another colonial strategy. The ransacking and destruction of Palmyra, the "Bride of the Desert" is an attempt to erase Syria's history, presumably to be replaced by a narrative of Western Wahhabist revisionism.

The strategy of "divide and conquer" is also a staple of colonizers. Currently, the West is supporting the Kurdish nationalist Party

---

32. *Ibid.*

(PYD) and its military wing (YPG)[33] in their efforts to annex Syrian land and to impose federalism on Syria. If successful, such efforts would serve to weaken Syria and to engineer conflicts between competing factions – another useful colonial tool.

The inability of the UN to deal with these illegal, genocidal colonial strategies is epitomized by a Facebook posting, dated November 20, 2016, wherein Martin discusses UN Special Envoy for Syria Staffan de Mistura's ridiculous proposal to cede control of East Aleppo to terrorists:[34]

> Aleppo, Syria Update: Nov 20, 2016: The American supported terrorists in East Aleppo shot out very heavy missiles into West Aleppo and struck an elementary school. 20 children and adults are dead. Over 120 severely injured. The injured and dead are at Razi Hospital in West Aleppo. It was a massacre. At the very same time in Damascus, the UN envoy to Syria, Staffan de Mistura's ridiculous proposal to cede control of East Aleppo to terrorists: was meeting with the Syrian Foreign Minister Walid Muallem. Mr Mistura, who has worked at the UN for 43 years, was offering the Syrian government a new plan to end the bloodshed in Aleppo. The UN and USA plan for Aleppo calls for the Syrian government to give East Aleppo to the TERRORISTS, who are supported by USA, but all aligned with Al-Qaeda, and have the same values and agenda as ISIS. The UN-USA plan is to establish a "Principality" in East Aleppo, which is independent of all of Syria. The UN-USA plan is to reward the people who chopped off the head of an 11-year-old boy, for no reason. To reward the terrorists who just yesterday slaughtered the unarmed civilians inside East Aleppo who had tried to make a run for it, to escape. They were shot in the back while running, trying to get to the safety and freedom of West Aleppo. Tell me, what should Syria tell the UN and USA? If the terrorists ask you to give up East New York City will you agree?

Martin's story is corroborated by a report, dated 28 November

33. PYD – Partiya Yekîtiya Demokrat, Kurdish Democratic Union Party; YPG – Yekîneyên Parastina Gel, People's Protection Units
34. Lilly Martin, Facebook post shared with friends, 20 November 2016.

2016, from Dr Nabil Antaki, a gastroenterologist based in West Aleppo:[35]

> At least, 4000 of our fellow citizens from East Aleppo, held hostage by the terrorists, have been able to flee with the help of the SAA and have taken temporary refuge in Jibrine. Others have been able to escape via Sheikh Maqsoud (Northern entry point into West Aleppo). Here are two pieces of good news.
>
> However there are two pieces of bad news and a concern: firstly, some of the fleeing East Aleppo civilians were killed by the terrorists and secondly, 12 civilians of West Aleppo were murdered today, by the rain of mortars still being launched by terrorists inside East Aleppo. We could say it was in reprisal for the SAA advances, but we have been subjected to these attacks daily for the last four years.
>
> What do we fear? Perhaps that Western governments and certain organisations will start campaigning for another cease-fire for "humanitarian reasons" (as they have done in the past). Or, that they will launch another media campaign in an attempt to halt the SAA campaign to liberate the people of East and West Aleppo from the clutches of the terrorist groups.
>
> Today, two media outlets were already asking me about the "humanitarian catastrophe" in East Aleppo. We await the inevitable disinformation that they will publish.

The degeneracy of the NATO terrorists is amplified by stories from liberated Aleppo. Beeley reported on 12 December 2016 that:[36]

> In Aleppo unable to upload any video or images.
>
> We spent much of yesterday in Hanano speaking with very recently liberated civilians. One lady I interviewed and filmed told me that her 8 year old daughter had died in Nusra Front prison 3 days before the liberation by SAA. Her eldest daughter had been chosen to be raped by the terrorists, saved by the

35. Vanessa Beeley. "Aleppo Updates: The Beginning of the End ~ Dr Nabil Antaki," 21st Century Wire. 28 November 2016.
(http://21stcenturywire.com/2016/11/28/aleppo-updates-the-beginning-of-the-end-dr-nabil-antaki/) Accessed 8 December 2016.
36. Vanessa Beeley, Facebook post shared globally, 12 December 2016.
(https://www.facebook.com/vanessa.beeley?hc_ref=NEWSFEED&fref=nf) Accessed 12 December 2016.

liberation. Her husband had been shot by the terrorists. She told me of a woman who had been begging the terrorists for food. They shot her in the mouth. She said terrorists had been murdering anyone who tried to leave Hanano via the humanitarian corridors and then blaming it on the Syrian government. She described all manner of torture and atrocities committed by these NATO "moderates".

The corporate media continues to spin the narratives even while these Syrian civilians thank them for coming to Hanano to tell their stories. That was heartbreaking. These Syrians incarcerated for 4 years by terrorists supported by these media criminals were so innocent of the media involvement in their pain and suffering.

I hope Channel 4 BBC CNN and many more are prosecuted as accessories to murder.

God bless the Syrian army and allies for the liberation.

Celebrating the liberation of Aleppo, at Aleppo University, December, 20, 2016 (Mhamad Kleit)

All of these colonial strategies are perpetuating an overseas holocaust as the West overrides international law and topples one government after another with a view to subjugating Iran, Russia, and

China as well. In "Unworthy Victims: Western wars have killed four million Muslims since 1990," Journalist Nafeez Ahmed argues that:[37]

> Total deaths from Western interventions in Iraq and Afghanistan since the 1990s – from direct killings and the longer-term impact of war-imposed deprivation – likely constitute around 4 million (2 million in Iraq from 1991-2003, plus 2 million from the 'war on terror'), and could be as high as 6–8 million people when accounting for higher avoidable death estimates in Afghanistan. Such figures could well be too high, but we'll never know for sure. US and UK armed forces, as a matter of policy, refuse to keep track of the civilian death toll of military operations – they are deemed an "irrelevant inconvenience."

Yet another form of suppression and control is the co-optation of the so-called "progressive left" as self-described "progressives" or "leftists" find themselves unwittingly supporting terrorism. Well-documented facts pertaining to the 9/11 wars, all supported by sustainable evidence, have barely made inroads into the collective consciousness of Western media consumers. Despite the presence of five years of sustainable evidence that contradicts the Western narratives, people still believe the "official" lies.

The consensus of ignorance is sustained by what Chossudovsky describes as an American Inquisition. Beneath the protection of this psychological operation, the engineered enemy is Islam, and the "Global War on Terrorism" has become a brand to disguise imperial wars of aggression as humanitarian. Thus, huge sums of public monies are diverted from worthwhile, domestic projects such as healthcare, schools and roads, to support a criminal Project for a New American Century that is globalizing death, poverty, and destruction as the US-led Empire tries to impose a unilateral model of control over the world. The US is said to be "exceptional," and therefore the rightful ruler. Manifest Destiny writ large.

Dissent is suppressed within the framework of corporate media

---

37. Nafeez Ahmed, "Unworthy victims: Western wars have killed four million Muslims since 1990" (http://www.middleeasteye.net/columns/unworthy-victims-western-wars-have-killed-four-million-muslims-1990-39149394). Accessed 8 December 2016.

monopolies. Predominant narratives are supported by corrupt non-governmental organizations – totally bereft of objectivity – and intelligence agency fronts. Real investigative journalism offering historical context and legitimate evidence are relegated to the fringes, far outside the domain of the broad-based "consensus of misunderstanding." To make matters even more dire for those who seek freedoms of expression and thought, President Obama signed into law, on December 23, 2016, the Countering Disinformation and Propaganda Act (Bill HR5181) as part of the annual National Defense Authorization Act.

According to Stephen Lendman in ""Big Brother" Watches Everyone in America: Obama Signs "Ministry of Truth" into Law" this means that "truth-telling on vital domestic and geopolitical issues is now considered fake news or Russian propaganda."

Independent investigative journalist Rick Sterling added to the condemnation of Bill HR5181 with this explanation, from his December 31st, 2016 article, "The Information War on Syria and Beyond":

> The passage of HR5181 "Countering Foreign Propaganda and Disinformation", suggests that the ruling powers seek to escalate suppression of news and analysis which runs counter to their narrative. Despite their current dominance in the media and information arena, that is not enough. They seek to further squelch opposing voices. The bill calls for "countering" and "refuting" what they deem to be propaganda and disinformation. A slush fund of $20M is provided to hire or reward "civil society groups, NGOs, journalists and private companies " who participate in the campaign.

The "Progressive Left" has been co-opted. So-called "progressives" (presumably unwittingly) support Canada's close relationships with Wahhabi Saudi Arabia, apartheid Israel, and even the foreign mercenaries currently invading Syria (i.e. ISIS and Al-Nusra Front/al-Qaeda).

The sources upon which the pretexts for war are built and perpetrated are taboo topics. The truth is seen as heresy, and fact-based narratives are derided as "conspiracy theories."

The deceptions are reinforced and shielded by police state legislation. Canada's Bill C-51 subverts citizens' freedoms, including freedoms of expression, and enables the apparatus of deception, as it protects governing polities that commit criminal acts. Constitutional lawyer Rocco Galati explained, during a rally in the summer of 2015, that Bill C-51 – which is now law – transforms Canada into a "fascist state, complete with a modern day Gestapo."

Galati explained:[38]

> It takes all our private information and shares it with all government agencies, including foreign governments. For some citizens that becomes an eventuality of torture and/or death when travelling abroad.
>
> It restricts arbitrarily who can travel.
>
> Freedom of expression and political criticism with respect to 'terrorism and the government's role' (becomes) a terrorist offence in itself. So words and thoughts become an act of terrorism under this Bill.
>
> It allows CSIS (Canadian Security Intelligence Service) to disrupt covertly constitutionally-protected rights of association, expression, and protest.
>
> It does all of this by taking away all and any transparent judicial oversight.

Galati adds that "We've entered into the final fascist state."

Thus, a firm foundation of lies that serve as a sanctified justification for global war and terror, remains strong.

But the stakes are high, as Western hegemony presses us closer and closer to a real prospect of widespread nuclear war. Already, the use of nuclear weapons is being normalized through the introduction of "mini-nukes" and the blurring of lines between conventional and nuclear war.

The taboos need to be lifted, and the repeated lies contradicted. Some of the more pernicious lies covering the escalating war on the democratic Syrian Arab Republic include unsubstantiated memes that fit neatly into the propagandists' toolbox of false representations,

---

38. Partial transcription of YouTube video, posted 30 May 2015, wherein Galati announces that he will challenge Bill C-51 in Federal Court.
(https://www.youtube.com/watch?v=-AhhC0sngPo) Accessed 5 December 2016.

and of projecting the West's crimes onto the victims (Syria and Syrians).

The war on Syria is not a "civil" war; the "uprising" was not "democratic"; Assad does not "starve his own people"; Assad, does not "bomb his own people"; Assad is the democratically elected President of Syria, and not a "brutal dictator."

Conclusive evidence demonstrates, and has demonstrated for years, that the war is an invasion by Western proxies, which include ISIS and al-Qaeda/Al-Nursra Front. There are no "moderates."

The initial uprisings were marred by foreign-backed violence perpetrated against innocent people, soldiers, and police. Peaceful grassroots protests were hijacked by these murderous foreign-backed elements (as was the case in Ukraine) – all consistent with "hybrid war" as developed by Andrew Korybko in *Hybrid Wars: The Indirect Adaptive Approach to Regime Change.*

The illegal sanctions imposed by the West – coupled with terrorist practices of theft and hoarding of humanitarian aid – are responsible for the starvation. This is well documented in the aforementioned testimonies.

Assad is a democratically elected reformer and hugely popular with Syrians, not a brutal dictator. Claims that he "kills his own people" were further debunked when the so-called "Caesar photos" evidence was proven to be a fraud. Tim Anderson explains in "The Dirty War On Syria: Barrel Bombs, Partisan sources, and War Propaganda" that:[39]

> When the Qatari monarchy (which has invested billions of dollars in the armed attacks on Syria) presents an anonymous, paid witness 'Caesar', with photos of numerous dead and tortured bodies, blaming the Syrian Army for 'industrial scale killing' (O'Toole 2014; Jalabi 2015), it should be plain that that 'evidence' is partisan and unreliable (Smith-Spark 2014; MMM 2014). The fact that this story was presented by a belligerent party just before a Geneva peace conference should give further

39. Tim Anderson. "The Dirty War on Syria: Barrel Bombs, Partisan Sources and War Propaganda." Global Research. 7 October 2015.
(http://www.globalresearch.ca/the-dirty-war-on-syria-barrel-bombs-partisan-sources-and-war-propaganda/5480362) Accessed 10 December 2016.

cause for suspicion. But without genuinely independent evidence to corroborate the witness we have no way of verifying in which year, circumstance or even which country the photos were taken. Those who finance and arm the sectarian groups have slaughtered hundreds of thousands in recent years, in the wars in Afghanistan, Iraq and Syria. There is no shortage of photos of dead bodies. The fact that Western media sources run these accusations, using lawyers (also paid by Qatar) to provide 'bootstrap' support (Cartalucci 2014; Murphy 2014), merely shows their limited understanding of independent evidence.

The delusions of the so-called "left" and "progressives" is exemplified by a piece from the Socialist Project: "Solidarity with the People of Syria! Build the Antiwar Movement!" where journalist Richard Fidler writes:[40]

> In that country, the rebel cities that rose up four years ago in revolt against the brutal Bashar al-Assad dictatorship are now under a genocidal siege, bombed and assaulted from the air by Assad's military, aided and abetted by Russian fighter jets and bombers. Their desperate fight for survival, if unsuccessful, will put paid to the Arab Spring and with it the potential for building a democratic, antiimperialist governmental alternative in the Middle East for an extended period to come. Socialists everywhere have every interest in supporting the Syrian people and opposing that war.

This inversion of the well-documented truth is commonly accepted by so-called "progressives" and "leftists."

The truth pierces the fog of lies and deceptions, and it is a necessary foundation for peace. Author Catherine Shakdam writes in "The Sound of Your Silence":[41]

> SHAFAQNA – Today silence has become more than a war crime. Today silence has become more than just the manifes-

---

40. Richard Fidler, "Solidarity with the People of Syria!: Build the Anitwar Movement!" The Bullet. Socialist Project, E-Bulletin No. 1332, 18 November, 2016. (http://www.socialistproject.ca/bullet/1332.php) Accessed 5 December 2016.
41. Catherine Shakdam. "The Sound of Your Silence," Shia News Association, 19 August 2016. (http://en.shafaqna.com/news/36383) Accessed 5 December 2016.

tation of our egocentrism and selfishness. Today silence has enabled, empowered and shielded oppressors and tyrants.

In *From Mecca to the plain of Karbala: Walking with the Holy household of the Prophet* Imam Husayn recites Farwa ibn Musayk Muradi:[42]

> If we have been victorious today it is not something new, because we have always gained victory and even if we are defeated, predominance and victory is ours; and truth is victorious in all circumstances, whether it wins or loses.

These lines underscore the importance of truth-telling if we are to achieve victory over the lies and crimes of Empire. Stated bluntly, Islam, correctly interpreted, is not the enemy. We are.

Shakdam explains in "The Walk of Light – Arbaeen Pilgrimage Rises a Great Resistance against Radicalism"[43] that:

> Arbaeen it needs to be said stands very much an offense to Wahhabism – this dogma the House of Saud has furiously promoted to assert its ascent to power. Arba'een it needs to be emphasized, actually speaks of this eternal struggle in between Good and Evil, Freedom and Slavery, Piety and Dogmatism.

Whereas the West supports the extremist Wahhabism of Saudi Arabia, the teachings of Islam contradict this ideology, and they certainly contradict the crimes of the mercenary terrorists infesting Syria.

It is known and documented, and has been for years, that the West and its allies support these un-Islamic terrorists to destroy and control other countries and their peoples. It is known and documented that the terrorists who behead, rape, and pillage their way through the Middle East and elsewhere are our proxies. We pay the bills, and we orchestrate the carnage.

---

42. Catherine Shakdam. From Mecca to the plain of Karbala: Walking with the Holy household of the Prophet. From a chapter entitled "Who was Imam Hussain." CreateSpace Independent Publishing, 14 October 2016.
43. Catherine Shakdam "The Walk of Light – Arbaeen Pilgrimage Rises a Great Resistance against Radicalism." American Herald Tribune. 19 November 2016. (http://ahtribune.com/religion/1344-arbaeen-radicalism.html) Accessed 8 December 2016.

Prof. Chossudovsky remarks in the preface to this book that:

> Everybody in Syria knows that Washington is behind the terrorists, that they are financed by the US (at tax payers' expense) and its allies, trained and recruited by America's Middle East partner. Saudi Arabia, Qatar, have been financing and training the ISIS–Daesh, al-Nusra terrorists on behalf of the United States. Israel is harboring the terrorists out of the occupied Golan Heights, NATO in liaison with the Turkish high command has since March 2011 been involved in coordinating the recruitment of the jihadist fighters dispatched to Syria.
>
> Moreover, the ISIS–Daesh brigades in both Syria and Iraq are integrated by Western special forces and military advisors.
>
> While all this is known to the Syrian people, Western public opinion is led to believe that the US is leading a 'counter-terrorism campaign' in Syria and Iraq against the Islamic State (ISIS–Daesh), an entity created and supported by US intelligence.

As NATO and its allies commit war crimes against non-belligerent Syria and Yemen, and Washington promises war and more war, we need to break the silence. Our political representatives no longer represent us.

Presumably, they too have been heavily propagandized and they believe the lies laundered by our criminal mainstream media. But ignorance is no longer a legitimate excuse.

In the case of Syria, we need to demand that our misleaders take immediately attainable steps to achieve peace, as outlined by the United States Peace Council:[44]

> We call on all activists in the peace movement to flood the emails and phone lines of the White House and the State Department and demand the following:
>
> 1. Stop all foreign efforts to force regime change in Syria:
>
>   a) Stop bombing Syrian economic infrastructure in the

---

44. "Syria: Let Us Make Our Collective Voice of Reason be Heard." *An Urgent Appeal by the U.S. Peace Council: To All of Our Friends in the Peace Movement.* U.S. Peace Council, 23 January 2016. (http://uspeacecouncil.org/?p=2826) Accessed 5 December 2016.

name of fighting ISIS.

b) Stop injecting foreign fighters into Syria.

c) Stop funding, organizing and arming the combatants in Syria.

2. Let the Syrians themselves decide the future of their country free of all foreign intervention:

a) Allow all truly moderate internal opposition groups and the Kurdish organizations to participate in the negotiations.

Exclude no segment of the Syrian population from peace negotiations.

Exclude all foreign opposition forces, as well as all terrorist organizations, from the negotiations.

3. Lift all sanctions on Syria. Provide humanitarian aid to the Syrian people. Help the Syrian refugees settle wherever they want – including back in Syria.

4. End all wars of aggression, all forms of foreign occupation, and all externally-generated regime change policies in the region.

None of the countries that we are threatening or attacking, including Russia, are real threats. General Petr Pavel, Chairman of the NATO Military Committee, acknowledged that, "It is not the aim of NATO to create a military barrier against broad-scale Russian aggression, because such aggression is not on the agenda and no intelligence assessment suggests such a thing."

The NATO military build-up is unnecessary and dangerous, as is the criminal war on Syria.

As I noted in "Fake Threats and Engineered Fears":[45]

> The 'Russian threat' is fake; there never was a 'Syria threat' (except that Syria insists on its sovereignty and territorial in-

45. Mark Taliano, "Fake threats and engineered fears," American Herald Tribune. 16 July 2016. (http://ahtribune.com/politics/1073-engineered-fears.html) Accessed 5 December 2016.

tegrity); and the 'terrorist threat' is a hoax, because we support the terrorists.

The 'humanitarian bombing' strategy is also a hoax, because ISIS territory expands when the U.S illegally bombs Syria.

Basically, everything we're hearing is fake. The government, and Soros et al funded "non-government organizations" (NGOs) are fake, not only because they aren't "non-governmental", but also because they're embedded with the terrorist invaders.

But the pursuit of truth and just peace is an uphill battle. The Pentagon's "Law of War" manual, for example, views the control and manipulation of information as a (legitimate) "soft power" weapon, and the US Department of Defense public relations/ propaganda budget alone is reported to be about $600,000,000 per year.

John Pilger reports in *The Coming War on China* that the Pentagon spends billions on fake news:[46]

> In 2014, under the rubric of "information dominance" – the jargon for media manipulation, or fake news, on which the Pentagon spends more than $4 billion – the Obama Administration launched a propaganda campaign that cast China, the world's greatest trading nation, as a threat to 'freedom of navigation'.

As responsible citizens, we need to reject the war lie and insist on truth and a just peace. Even if the truth "loses" and warmongers are elected, truth still "wins" because it engaged with the enemy, despite the odds.

---

46. John Pilger. "The Coming War on China: Nuclear War is No Longer a Shadow," Global Research, 3 December 2016. (http://www.globalresearch.ca/the-coming-war-on-china-nuclear-war-is-no-longer-a-shadow/5560156) Accessed 8 December 2016.

CHAPTER IV
Western Crimes against International Law and Order

Genocidal corporate media presstitutes follow the all-too-familiar script of blaming the victim for the crimes perpetrated by aggressor nations, as it creates war propaganda. NATO terrorists, for example, are invading and occupying Syria, and the Syrian government is blamed for the ensuing disasters, but the presstitutes omit this from their narratives and instead find creative ways to blame the al-Assad government whose duty it is to protect Syria, its sovereignty, and its territorial integrity. When terrorists are occupying cities, as they do in Syria, innocent people will always be victimized, including during government operations to clear out the terrorist infestations, but the presstitutes blame the Syrian government, not the NATO terrorists. Many Syrians would prefer that President al-Assad be harsher with the terrorists. In a November 17, 2016 interview, in French, with KAIROS Productions, Dr. Nabil Antaki, a resident of government-secured West Aleppo, expressed his exasperation at being bombed and terrorized from the occupied areas for more than four years. He explained that every day, for four and a half years, terrorists had attacked Aleppo citizens with mortars and with gas canisters filled with explosives and nails. He also explained that the water was cut for three years, forcing residents to dig wells inside the city, and that there were electricity cuts as well.

President al-Assad is fraudulently demonized for a war perpetrated by aggressors who are tasked with destroying Syria so the West can further the destruction under a fraudulent Responsibility to Protect mandate or a "No Fly Zone" wherein the criminal West promises to save Syrians from the West's own terrorists. It is basically a mafia-style protection racket: If al-Assad steps down, we'll "protect you" and replace him with a Wahhabi stooge government, and everyone will be happy.

The reality of course, is that if the Western terrorists win the war and

Syria will be totally destroyed, much like Libya, Iraq, and the Ukraine. The crimes of the aggressors have been well documented for years, and all but ignored by the mainstream media.

The earlier referenced Defense Intelligence Agency document 14-L-0552/DIA indicated that US-supported ISIS as a strategic asset and that the US aided the transferral of weapons from Libya to Syria. In an interview with Mehdi Hasan, Michael T. Flynn, former director of the Defense Intelligence Agency, acknowledged US support for the terrorists in Syria:[47]

> *Mehdi Hasan*: In 2012, your agency was saying, quote: "The Salafists, the Muslim Brotherhood and al-Qaeda in Iraq are the major forces driving the insurgency in Syria." In 2012, the US was helping coordinate arms transfers to those same groups. Why did you not stop that, if you're worried about the rise of quote, unquote, "Islamic extremism"?
>
> *Michael Flynn*: Yeah, I, I mean, I hate to say it's not my job but that – my job was to ensure that the accuracy of our intelligence that was being presented was as good as it could be, and I will tell you, it goes before 2012.

The *New York Times*, another propaganda outlet, cannot help but reveal the truth, even if indirectly, when, in a 2016 article, "CIA Arms for Syrian Rebels Supplied Black Market, Officials Say"[48] it acknowledged that "Weapons shipped into Jordan by the Central Intelligence Agency and Saudi Arabia (were) intended for Syrian rebels"

A single packing list of weapons transferred to terrorists indicates the magnitude of the terrorist-arming operation:[49]

---

47. "Transcript: Michael Flynn on ISIL." Interview with Mehdi Hasan. Head to Head, Al Jazeera. 13 January 2016. (http://www.aljazeera.com/programmes/headto-head/2016/01/transcript-michael-flynn-160104174144334.html) Accessed 8 December 2016.

48. Mark Mazzetti and Ali Younes. "C.I.A. Arms for Syrian Rebels Supplied Black Market, Officials Say," *New York Times*, 26 June 2016. (http://www.nytimes.com/2016/06/27/world/middleeast/cia-arms-for-syrian-rebels-supplied-black-market-officials-say.html) Accessed 8 December 2016.

49. Jeremy Binnie and Neil Gibson. "Infantry Weapons: US arms shipment to Syrian rebels detailed." IHS Jane's Defence Weekly. 8 April 2016. (http://www.janes.com/article/59374/us-arms-shipment-to-syrian-rebels-detailed) Accessed 10 December 2016.

Simplified packing list for December 2015 arms shipment

Type	Weight (kg)		
	Aqaba	Agalar	Total
7.62x39 mm	85,190	48,998	134,188
7.62x54 mm	58,752	8,652	67,404
12.7 mm	81,468.40	36,713	118,181
14.5 mm	196,233.76	173,447	369,681
82 mm	53,885.34		53,885
PG-7VM	0.00	68,600	68,600
PG-7VT	36,795	88,224.00	125,019
9M111M	13,540	8,153	21,693
AK-47 & DShK*	12,250		12,250
AK-47 & PKM*		6,540	6,540
PKM	6,340		6,340
DShK & RPG-7*		3,585	3,585
RPG-7	4,120		4,120
Faktoria launchers	2,421.60	298	2,720
Total	550,996	443,210	994,206

* The packing list merged some categories

More recently, with the liberation of Aleppo in late December, 2016, warehouses filled with NATO-supplied weapons were discovered.

Meanwhile, UN Security Council Resolution 1373, section 2(a), states clearly that all States shall:[50] "Refrain from providing any form of support, active or passive, to entities or persons involved in terrorist acts, including by suppressing recruitment of members of terrorist groups and eliminating the supply of weapons to terrorists."

All of this evidence assigns guilt directly to the West for the disaster befalling Syria. The West's actions contradict international law and they expose the lies of the presstitute media that typically vilifies the al-Assad government rather than the real perpetrators.

Yet another article, "U.S. Relies Heavily on Saudi Money to Support Syrian Rebels,"[51] indicates that the West is also behind the financing of the terrorists. The writers revel that:

50. United Nations Security Council Resolution 1373, S/RES/1373 (2001), Adopted by the Security Council at its 4385th meeting, on 28 September 2001.(https://www.unodc.org/pdf/crime/terrorism/res_1373_english.pdf) Accessed 10 December 2016.
51. Mark Mazzetti and Matt Apuzzo. "U.S. Relies Heavily on Saudi Money to Support Syrian Rebels," New York Times. 23 January 2016. (http://www.nytimes.com/2016/01/24/world/middleeast/us-relies-heavily-on-saudi-money-to-support-syrian-rebels.html) Accessed 8 December 2016.

When President Obama secretly authorized the CIA to begin arming Syria's embattled rebels in 2013, the spy agency knew it would have a willing partner to help pay for the covert operation. It was the same partner the CIA has relied on for decades for money and discretion in far-off conflicts: the Kingdom of Saudi Arabia.

American made weapons found when Al Nusra left. Photo: Syrian Arab Army

Since then, the CIA and its Saudi counterpart have maintained an unusual arrangement for the rebel-training mission, which the Americans have code-named Timber Sycamore. Under the deal, current and former Administration officials said, the Saudis contribute both weapons and large sums of money, and the CIA takes the lead in training the rebels on AK-47 assault rifles and tank-destroying missiles.

Financing terrorists is also a violation of UN Resolutions (and international law). UN Resolution 2199 urges:[52]

States to prevent the terrorist groups from gaining access to international financial institutions and reaffirmed States' ob-

---

52. "Unanimously Adopting Resolution 2199 (2015), Security Council Condemns Trade with Al-Qaida Associated Groups, Threatens Further Targeted Sanctions," Security Council, 7379th Meeting. SC/11775. United Nations Meetings Coverage and Press Releases. 12 February 2015.
(http://www.un.org/press/en/2015/sc11775.doc.htm) Accessed 8 December 2016.

ligations to prevent the groups from acquiring arms and related materiel, along with its call to enhance coordination at the national, regional and international level for that purpose.

Add to this the fact that Israel's Defense Minister Moshe Ya'alon admitted that he would prefer ISIS to the Syrian government, which he calls an Iranian proxy,[53] and we see that the presstitute narratives are falling apart yet again.

Dr Bouthaina Shaaban, al-Assad's Political and Media Advisor, assesses the damage committed by Western media outlets that propagate false narratives about Syria:[54]

> What I would like to say is that the false narrative propagated about Syria was as dangerous to the Syrian people and to the safety and security of Syrians, as the acts perpetrated by terrorists, because it isolated the reality in Syria from the public understanding in the West and in the world at large, and it prevented the creation of a level of understanding between Western countries and the Syrian people about what is going on.

What will be the next story advanced by the media to account for the clear criminality of the West and its terrorists? How many more thousands of innocent people will lose their lives because of Western lies.

---

53. Judah Ari Gross. "Ya'alon: I would prefer Islamic State to Iran in Syria" The Times of Israel. 19 January 2016. (http://www.timesofisrael.com/yaalon-i-would-prefer-islamic-state-to-iran-in-syria/) Accessed 10 December 2016.

54. Dr Bouthaina Shaaban "Reconstruction with Syrian characteristics – rebuilding a truly diverse and more secure world based on the lessons of the Syrian experience," Forum for a New Paradigm. Schiller Institute's Berlin International Conference, 25-26 June 2016.
(http://newparadigm.schillerinstitute.com/media/her-excellency-dr-bouthaina-shabaan-reconstruction-with-syrian-characteristics-rebuilding-a-truly-diverse-and-more-secure-world-based-on-the-lessons-of-the-syrian-experience/) Accessed 10 December 2016.

CHAPTER V
Lies and Crimes:
Media Manipulation and Societal Oppression

It is amply documented that the "West," including US-led NATO, the Persian Gulf monarchies and Israel, are waging a proxy war against Syria. ISIS–Daesh is the designated enemy, but it has long been publicly acknowledged that the real enemy is President al-Assad of Syria, not ISIS. All of the invading, un-Islamic mercenary terrorists are the West's strategic assets, including ISIS. Engineered islamophobia is all part of Western psychological operations to demonize all Muslims and create fear, racism, and hatred – vital components for illegal wars of aggression.

Empire seeks to replace the democratic, pluralist, progressive government of President al-Assad with a Wahhabi-inspired, compliant, stooge government.

We have witnessed Empire's genocidal handiwork in Iraq, Libya, Ukraine and beyond – all part of a project for global dominance, globalized war, and globalized poverty. But Syria and its allies, including Russia and Iran, have drawn a red-line with Syria. Empire's unipolar ambitions are being frustrated on Syrian soil.

The war is not a "clash of civilizations" as some warmongers might profess; it is a clash of one civilization, Syria's, against Western barbarism.

Criminal mainstream messaging, however, has created a state of mass political imbecilization amongst Western media consumers. In a classic case of "reverse-projection," people's engineered perceptions present President al-Assad and Syrians as the "bad guys," while the invading terrorists are viewed as the "good guys."

Repeated messaging of these false narratives, coupled with sophisticated confusion-mongering, continues to weld these lies into the collective political consciousness of Western media consumers.

How did the "Establishment" orchestrate such a coup?

Ostensibly neutral information sources are not neutral at all. So-called "non-governmental organizations" – referenced earlier – and very governmental sources such as the National Endowment for Democracy, the CIA, Mossad, etc., as well as oligarch-funded foundations, are all embedded with the terrorists, and these are the sources that are the foundation for corporate/mainstream media "news" stories.

The White Helmets, the Syrian Observatory for Human Rights, and Avaaz are just a few of the many corrupt NGOs lying about the war on Syria. Tim Anderson explains in "Interview with Prof. Tim Anderson: 'NATO's Dirty War on Syria'" that:[55]

> (t)he 'White Helmets' are a Wall Street creation, funded and led by the US and the UK, to give 'humanitarian' cover to the al-Qaeda groups they support. This fake NGO participates directly in the sectarian terrorist campaigns, helping with the war propaganda that terrorist fighters are 'civilians', in an attempt to de-legitimize the resistance of the Syrian Army and its allies.

Independent journalist Eva Bartlett noted at a 9 December 2016 Press briefing by the Syrian Mission at the United Nations that "No one in East Aleppo has heard of them" (the White Helmets) thus further exposing the West's apparatus of lies.[56]

In a 5 December 2016, Facebook posting, Donna Nasser, a member of the US Peace Council wrote:[57]

---

55. Vanessa Beeley. "Interview with Prof. Tim Anderson: NATO's Dirty War on Syria," 21st Century Wire. 25 June 2016. (http://21stcenturywire.com/2016/06/25/interview-with-prof-tim-anderson-natos-dirty-war-on-syria/) Accessed 8 December 2016.
56. "Permanent Mission of the Syrian Arab Republic to the United Nations – Press Conference, 9 December 2016." Press Briefing by Syrian Mission. Speakers, including Eva Bartlett, Independent Canadian Journalist. United Nations Webcast. 9 December 2016. (http://webtv.un.org/watch/permanent-mission-of-the-syrian-arab-republic-to-the-united-nations-press-conference-9-december-2016/5241732190001#full-text) Accessed 10 December 2016.
57. Donna Nassor. Facebook post shared globally on The Full Circle Project, 5 December 2016 at 17:56. (https://www.facebook.com/fullspectrumresponse/) Accessed 8 December 2016.

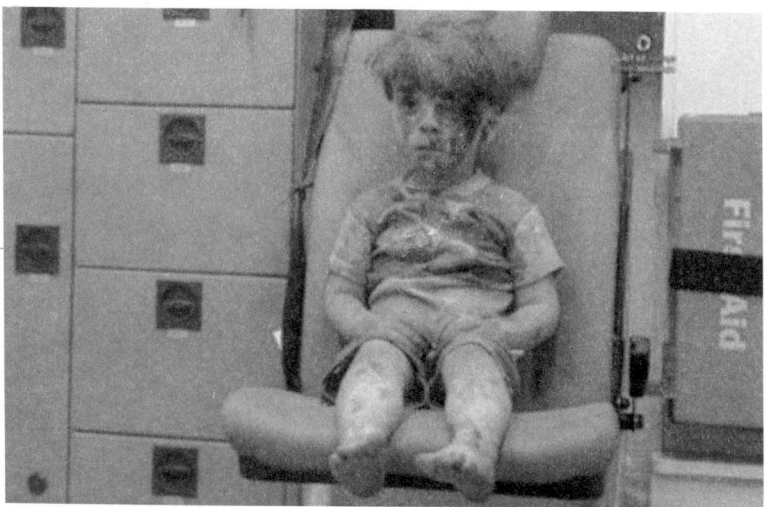

The "White Helmets" stage theatrical productions as part of the terrorists' apparatus of deception. (Aleppo Media Centre)

If the US–NATO coalition had not sent terrorists into Syria in this proxy war, Assad wouldn't have to be making tough decisions about how to preserve the lives of Syrians while he works to rid the country of the mercenaries. The Syrian Arab Army has been doing an amazing job and from the reactions I witnessed from the Syrian public when I was there, the appreciation for the SAA is representative of the majority.

The sooner the terrorists are gone, the sooner Assad and the Syrian people can heal, rebuild, and decide where to go from here. FYI – Assad told us when we met with him that he hopes the refugees will return as soon as possible. Once this proxy war has ended that may be possible.

Please don't allow yourselves to be taken in by the propaganda machine still trying to manipulate your thoughts about Syria. Take the time to seek truth from reliable sources who have actually been in Syria during these difficult times. Internalizing second and third-hand reports from so-called experts who continue to rely on reports from NGO's that receive funding from sources with their own agenda does not make you an expert. It just keeps you misinformed.

Add to this Qatari-based Al Jazeera, and Western media's method of trotting out "experts" who have conflicts of interest but who nevertheless pose as "neutral" sources of information, and we see that the media serves as an agency for imperial war rather than as an agency for truth and justice.

Meanwhile, voices of truth, justice and peace are suppressed. Anderson recently posted these words:[58]

> In my country (Australia) we have seen five years of a near monolithic war narrative on Syria, and associated wartime censorship of dissenting views. Although I have probably written more than any other Australian academic on the conflict in Syria, I have been effectively black-listed from the Australian corporate and state media, because what I say does not fit the official line.

Lies of omission are amongst the most pernicious in the apparatus of Western deceptions.

For example, millions of Shia Muslims from dozens of countries recently made a pilgrimage to Karbala, Iraq for Arba'een, to mourn the martyrdom in 680 AD of Imam Husayn, whose teachings of truth, piety and tolerance contradicted those of the tyrant Yazid, just as they contradict the "teachings" of ISIS mercenaries today. Such a transformative and relevant event, the world's largest annual gathering, would have figured prominently in the mainstream media, if mainstream media served our national and international interests instead of serving the interests of special groups, namely the war profiteers.

Similar lies of omission impact Syria's Christian communities. Sarah Abdallah noted in an 8 December 2016 Facebook comment that:[59] "Beautiful: Christians celebrate mass in the Greek-Melkite Cathedral of Our Lady of Peace in Old Homs today. There would be no mass, nor churches if Al-Qaeda groups still ruled the Old City."

North American Christians seem unaware that the terrorist proxies supported by the West commit genocide against Christians.

---

58. Tim Anderson, Facebook post, dated 7 July 2016. (https://www.facebook.com/timand2037/posts/10208647842246424) Accessed 5 December 2015.
59. Sarah Abdallah. Facebook post shared globally. 8 December 2016, 11:44.

Not only are the lies enabling the siege of Syria and its peoples, but they are also propelling us blindly towards a possibly cataclysmic nuclear war against Russia and its allies. The stakes are high, and there are ominous forebodings that Washington-based warmongering circles – namely the military–industrial complex – are intent on provoking the unthinkable, cataclysmic nuclear warfare.

The "Strategic Deterrent Coalition," a non-profit organization with funding from war-profiteering companies such as Boeing, Northrop Grumman, Orbital ATK, and BAE Systems, is one such circle. It aims to "educate" decision-makers and "build a consensus" in favour of the pre-emptive/first-strike use of nuclear weapons.[60]

The jargon sounds almost benign but the premise upon which the fear-mongering is based is absurd. Professor Michel Chossudovsky explains in "'The Doomsday Forum': Senior Military, Nuclear Weapons Officials Convene … America's '$1 Trillion Nuclear Weapons Plan'. Take out Russia, Iran and North Korea?"[61]

> Theatre of the absurd: the US is intent upon using nuclear weapons as a means of self-defence against al-Qaeda and ISIS under the Administration's counter-terrorism initiative:
>
>> And the United States is part of an international campaign against violent extremist organizations groups 'seeking to destroy our democratic way of life.'
>>
>> To effectively keep adversaries and potential adversaries in check, America must maintain 'a safe, secure, effective and ready nuclear deterrent.'
>>
>> Lest we forget, al-Qaeda was created by the CIA and the ISIS is supported and funded by two of America's staunchest allies: Turkey and Saudi Arabia.

---

60. "America must maintain a safe, secure and effective strategic nuclear deterrent to assure its safety and security now and for the future." Position Paper on the Nuclear Deterrent. Strategic Deterrent Coalition. 2013 – 2016. (http://sdc-usa.org/position-paper/) Accessed 10 December 2016.
61. Michel Chossudovsky. "'The Doomsday Forum': Senior Military, Nuclear Weapons Officials Convene… America's "$1 Trillion Nuclear Weapons Plan". Take out Russia, Iran and North Korea?"" Global Research. 8 July 2016. (http://www.globalresearch.ca/the-doomsday-forum-senior-military-nuclear-weapons-officials-convene-americas-1-trillion-nuclear-weapons-plan/5534549) Accessed 8 December 2016.

In fact, the entire "War on Terror" constitutes the "Theater of the Absurd," since the stated enemies of the "West" (i.e. al-Qaeda/Al-Nusra Front, ISIS, and all the terrorists invading Syria) are supported by the West, the Gulf monarchies, NATO and Israel.

Instead of building a consensus for war and first-strike nuclear attacks, we need to build a consensus for truth, justice, and peace.

As a first step, we would do well to boycott toxic mainstream media messaging, which favours lies, injustice, and war.

Beneath the "liberal" veneer, our government supports Wahhabism, misogyny, terrorism, madrassa/Wahhabi schools, death squads, death cults and civilian massacres.

Instead of furthering the causes of knowledge, growth, humanity and civilization, we are fostering barbarity and ignorance.

These are the forces growing in the Middle East thanks to Canada's complicity in NATO, and its support for Wahhabi Saudi Arabia and the mercenary terrorists invading and occupying Syria.

Islam is not the root of the destruction in the Middle East; we are.

All of this has been proven beyond doubt, and yet Canada remains transfixed by fabricated mainstream media stories that serve as the propaganda apparatus for Western-supported terrorists, including ISIS and all the terrorists invading Syria. The deception is broad-based and institutionalized. Mainstream media is basically an arm of the warmongering Establishment, but the truth eventually emerges. We know that the 935 pretexts leading to the illegal invasion of Iraq were blatant lies. We know that the Libyan invasion was based on lies, and we know that the narratives about Syria are false.

But even the mainstream media occasionally cracks its veneer to make relatively minor admissions. An 11 September 2016 article entitled "BBC quietly sneaks out correction admitting it blatantly lied in the run-up to war in Syria" details how the BBC falsely described a peaceful anti-war protest, with a view to smearing anti-war protestors and engineering consent for war. BBC radio acknowledges that:[62]

---

62. Patrick George "BBC quietly sneaks out correction admitting it blatantly lied in the run-up to war in Syria" Evolve Politics. 11 September 2016. (http://evolvepolitics.com/bbc-quietly-sneaks-correction-admitting-blatantly-lied-run-war-syria/) Accessed 8 December 2015.

Two listeners complained that the programme had inaccurately reported that a peaceful vigil in Walthamstow, in protest against the decision to bomb targets in Syria, had targeted the home of the local MP, Stella Creasy, and had been part of a pattern of intimidation towards Labour MPs who had supported the decision. The claim that the demonstration had targeted Ms Creasy's home, and the implication that it was intimidatory in nature, originated from a single Facebook posting which later proved to be misleading (the demonstration's destination was Ms Creasy's constituency office, which was unoccupied at the time, not her home, and it was peaceful).

This, of course, is relatively insignificant compared to the "Big Lies", but it does provide a peek into the criminality of the media.

A more significant lie that would fall under the category of "Big Lie" would be the mainstream media depiction in late November 2016 of the situation in Aleppo. Whereas local videos and testimonies from Syrians living in East Aleppo demonstrate clearly that the former captives were overjoyed to be liberated from the terrorist occupation, mainstream media would have us believe that the opposite is true, and that it is the Syrian Arab Army that is to be feared.

War lies are not insignificant. Christopher Black explains in "NATO War Propaganda: A Danger To World Peace" that propaganda which incites aggressive war (i.e. illegal invasions) was codified by the International Covenant on Civil and Political Rights, and was adopted by the General Assembly of the United Nations in 1966. Article 20 states:[63]

1. Any propaganda for war shall be prohibited by law;

2. Any advocacy of national, racial, religious hatred that constitutes incitement to discrimination, hostility, or violence shall be prohibited by law.

Most Canadians, unfortunately, remain captured by the propaganda and are immune to publicly available, evidence-based re-

63. Christopher Black. "NATO War Propaganda: A Danger to World Peace," *New Eastern Outlook*. 13 March 2015. (http://journal-neo.org/2015/03/13/nato-war-propaganda-a-danger-to-world-peace/) Accessed 8 December 2016.

search, as they passively accept the comforting lies and illusions.

We are taught to hate Islam, and tacitly embrace Saudi Wahhabism, even as the truth resides in the genuine teachings of Islam – and all the world's religions – as best represented by the culture of Syria and its peoples, our fabricated "enemy."

The voice of truth and evidence-based reality is an enduring, slow-burning flame, not easily extinguished; unlike its counterparts, lies and deceptions, which burn intensely for a time but then devours itself.

Aleppo resident Dr. Nabil Antaki explained that, "every day, for four and a half years, terrorists had attacked Aleppo citizens with mortars and with gas canisters filled with explosives and nails."

The truth in Syria is that there are no "moderate rebels" and that the US is not against gun-toting terrorists who occupy sections of Syria, murder civilians, launch Hell-Cannon ordnances, launch toxic/poison gas rockets, and attempt to impose Wahhabist teachings in occupied areas. Professor Chossudovsky explains that:[64]

> US counter-terrorism bombing campaign under 'Operation Inherent Resolve' does not target terrorists. Quite the opposite.

64. Michel Chossudovsky. "America's 'Humanitarian Massacre'of Syrian Civilians: The 'Counter-Terrorism' Campaign Is Directed against the Syrian People," Global Research. 31 July 2016. (http://www.globalresearch.ca/americas-humanitarian-massacre-of-syrian-civilians-the-counter-terrorism-campaign-is-directed-against-the-syrian-people/5538877) Accessed 8 December 2016.

Both ISIS–Daesh and Al-Nusra are protected by the US-led coalition. The forbidden truth is that the counter-terrorism campaign is directed against the Syrian people.

A recent Wikileaks document adds more evidence to a mountain of already-existing evidence that demonstrates that the West arms and supports the terrorists. Julian Assange explains in a *Democracy Now* interview that:[65]

> [T]he disastrous, absolutely disastrous intervention in Libya, the destruction of the Gaddafi government, which led to the occupation of ISIS of large segments of that country, weapons flows going over to Syria, being pushed by Hillary Clinton, into jihadists within Syria, including ISIS, that's there in those emails. There's more than 1,700 emails in Hillary Clinton's collection that we have released, just about Libya alone.

The terrorists are proxies/strategic assets for the West. We create them, lead them, support their infrastructure, and sustain them. Western, open-sourced documentation proves this. As I've written elsewhere:[66]

> The ugly truth about the genocidal Western designs for Syria (has been) well documented for years by sources including former Defense Intelligence Agency chief Michael Flynn, by Generals Dempsey, and Clark, by Vice-President Biden, and by publicly available Defense Intelligence Agency documents, as well as from other open-source documents.

A declassified intelligence report, Defense Intelligence Agency document 14-L-0552/DIA/287-293, dated 12 August 2012 and re-

---

65. "Assange: Why I Created WikiLeaks' Searchable Database of 30,000 Emails from Clinton's Private Server"" Transcript of Interview with Juan González. Democracy Now. 25 July 2016 (https://www.democracynow.org/2016/7/25/assange_why_i_created_wikileaks_searchable) Accessed 5 December 2016.
66. Mark Taliano. "Outrageous crimes and genocide protected by Western lies and duplicity," American Herald Tribune. 22 July 2016. (http://ahtribune.com/human-rights/1086-outrageous-crimes.html) Accessed 8 December 2016.

leased 18 May 2015, shows that the rise of ISIS was seen as a strategic asset by the United States.[67] On page 289, the document states, in part, that:

A. Internally, events are taking a clear sectarian direction.

B. The Salafist, – the Muslim Brotherhood and AQI (al-Qaeda in Iraq) are the major forces driving the insurgency in Syria.

THE GENERAL SITUATION:

A. INTERNALLY, EVENTS ARE TAKING A CLEAR SECTARIAN DIRECTION.

B. THE SALAFIST,- THE MUSLIM BROTHERHOOD, AND AQI ARE THE MAJOR FORCES DRIVING THE INSURGENCY IN SYRIA.

C. THE WEST, GULF COUNTRIES, AND TURKEY SUPPORT THE OPPOSITION WHILE RUSSIA. CHINA. AND IRAN SUPPORT THE REGIME.

[>X1) Sec 1. 4 (c),(b)(1) Sec. 1 4 (d)

E. THE REGIME'S PRIORITY IS TO CONCENTRATE ITS PRESENCE IN AREAS ALONG THE COAST (TARTUS, AND LATAKJA); HOWEVER, IT HAS NOT ABANDONED HOMS BECAUSE IT CONTROLS THE MAJOR TRANSPORTATION ROUTES IN SYRIA. THE REGIME DECREASED ITS CONCENTRATION IN AREAS ADJACENT TO THE IRAQI BORDERS (AL HASAKA AND DER ZOR).

3. AL   QAEDA- IRAQ (AQI):

A. AQI IS FAMILIAR WITH SYRIA. AQI TRAINED IN SYRIA AND THEN INFILTRATED INTO IRAQ.

B. AQI SUPPORTED THE SYRIAN OPPOSITION FROM THE BEGINNING, BOTH IDEOLOGICALLY AND THROUG H THE MEDIA. AQI DECLARED ITS OPPOSITION OF ASSAD'S GOVERNMENT BECAUSE IT CONSIDERED IT A SECTARIAN REGIME TARGETING SUNNIS.

C. AQI CONDUCTED A NUMBER OF OPERATIONS IN SEVERAL SYRIAN CITIES UNDER THE NAME OF JAISH AL NUSRA (VICTORIOUS ARMY), ONE OF ITS AFFILIATES.

D. AQI, THROUGH THE SPOKESMAN OF THE ISLAMIC STATE OF IRAQ (ISi), ABU MUHAMMAD AL ADNANI, DECLARED THE SYRIAN REGIME AS THE SPEARHEAD OF WHAT HE IS NAMING JIBHA AL RUWAFDII (FOREFRONT OF THE SHUTES) BECAUSE OF ITS (THE SYRIAN REGIME) DECLARATION OF WAR ON THE SUNNIS. ADDm ONALLY, HE IS CALLING ON THE SUNNIS IN IRAQ, ESPECIALLY THE TRIBES IN THE BORDER REGIONS (BETWEEN IRAQ AND SYRIA), TO WAGE WAR AGAINST THE SYRIAN REGIME, REGARDING SYRIA AS AN INFIDEL REGIME FOR ITS SUPPORT TO THE INFIDEL PARTY HEZBOLLAH, AND OTHER REGIMES HE

14-L-0552/DIA/

67. Defense Intelligence Agency document 14-L-0552/DIA/287-293, dated 12 August 2012, r‍ leased 18 May 2015. Pages 287–293 of the declassified report can be found at Judicial Wate (http://www.judicialwatch.org/document-archive/pgs-287-293-291-jw-v-dod-and-state-14-812 Accessed 10 December 2016.

C. The West, Gulf countries, and Turkey support the opposition while Russia, China and Iran support the Regime.

The document above and below[68] confirm that the US sees al-Qaeda as allies.

UNCLASSIFIED U.S. Department of State Case No. F-2014-20439 Doc No. C05789138 Date: 10/30/2015

RELEASE IN FULL

From:	Sullivan, Jacob J <SullivanJJ@state.gov>
Sent:	Sunday, February 12, 2012 4:01 PM
To:	H
Subject:	Fw: SPOT REPORT 02/12/II (SBU)

See last item - AQ is on our side in Syria.

Otherwise, things have basically turned out as expected.

In addition to the aforementioned admissions, Chossudovsky notes in "Five Years Ago: The US-NATO-Israel Sponsored Al-Qaeda Insurgency in Syria. Who was Behind the 2011 'Protest Movement'?" that:[69]

From Day One, the Islamist "freedom fighters" were supported, trained and equipped by NATO and Turkey's High Command. According to Israeli intelligence sources (Debka, August 14, 2011):

NATO headquarters in Brussels and the Turkish high command are meanwhile drawing up plans for their first military step in Syria, which is to arm the rebels with

68. Email from Jacob J Sullivan to "H" (Hillary Clinton), 12 February 2012. Unclassified US Department of State Case No. F-2014-20439, Document No. C05789138 Date: 10/30/2015. Wikileaks. (https://wikileaks.org/clinton-emails/Clinton_Email_October_Release/C05789138.pdf) Accessed 10 December 2016.
69. Michel Chossudovsky. "Five Years Ago: The US-NATO-Israel Sponsored Al Qaeda Insurgency in Syria. Who Was Behind The 2011 'Protest Movement'?" Global Research. 3 May 2011. (http://www.globalresearch.ca/syria-who-is-behind-the-protest-movement-fabricating-a-pretext-for-a-us-nato-humanitarian-intervention/24591) Accessed 5 December 2015.

> weapons for combating the tanks and helicopters spear-
> heading the Assad regime's crackdown on dissent. …
> NATO strategists are thinking more in terms of pouring
> large quantities of anti-tank and anti-air rockets, mortars
> and heavy machine guns into the protest centers for
> beating back the government armored forces. (DE-
> BKAfile, NATO to give rebels anti- tank weapons, Au-
> gust 14, 2011)

> This initiative, which was also supported by Saudi Ara-
> bia and Qatar, involved a process of organized recruit-
> ment of thousands of jihadist "freedom fighters",
> reminiscent of the enlistment of Mujahedeen to wage
> the CIA's jihad (holy war) in the heyday of the Soviet-
> Afghan war …

Chossudovsky also explains in "Bill Clinton Worked Hand in Glove with Al Qaeda: 'Helped Turn Bosnia into Militant Islamic Base'" that:[70]

> In retrospect, the Obama Administration's covert support
> of the ISIS in Syria and Iraq bears a canny resemblance to the
> Clinton Administration's support of the Militant Islamic Base
> in Bosnia and Kosovo. What this suggests is that US intelli-
> gence rather than the White House and the State Department
> determine the main thrust of US foreign policy, which consists
> in supporting and financing 'Jihadist' terrorist organizations
> with a view to destabilizing sovereign countries.

Historical memory teaches us that the dirty war against Syria is consistent with previous illegal wars of aggression and Western-sourced evidence demonstrates beyond a reasonable doubt that we are, yet again, the terrorists.

Western media consumers need to reject the fabricated main-stream media news stories – allied as they are to the terrorist cause

---

70. Michel Chossudovsky. "Bill Clinton Worked Hand in Glove with Al Qaeda: 'Helped Turn Bosnia into Militant Islamic Base'" Global Research, 3 November 2016. (http://www.globalresearch.ca/bill-clinton-worked-hand-in-glove-with-al-qaeda-helped-turn-bosnia-into-militant-islamic-base/5474094) Accessed 5 December 2016.

– and embrace evidence-based documentation instead. We also need to learn from history and avoid perpetrating the same deadly mistakes. We can no longer allow history to "repeat itself."

Fake notions of humanitarianism and a constant diet of war lies and manipulations lend themselves to a collective mindset which obliterates "yesterday."

The West's ongoing impunity as it continues to perpetrate genocide in Iraq should alert us to the dangers of repeated offenses elsewhere.Recent evidence has emerged, for example, that terrorists in East Aleppo committed mass slaughters and torture. In a December 28, 2016 article, "Syria-Gate: NATO Weaponry and Personnel in East Aleppo", Syrian MP Fares Shebabi explained,

> **So the terrorists left the city completely?**
> – Yes, but before they left they executed more than hundred Syrian soldiers and hundreds of civilians. We found their bodies. This is all documented. Any international independent investigation can see and check the evidence of these terrorist crimes.

The torture and slaughter of people in occupied territories is consistent with Western/CIA strategies. Writers Doug Valentine and Nicholas J.S. Davies wrote in "War Crimes as Policy" (May 31, 2013) :

> In February the Guardian and BBC Arabic unveiled a documentary exploring the role of retired Colonel James Steele in the recruitment, training and initial deployments of the CIA advised and funded Special Police Commandos in Iraq.
> The documentary tells how the Commandos tortured and murdered tens of thousands of Iraqi men and boys. But the Commandos were only one of America's many weapons of mass destruction in Iraq. Along with US military forces – which murdered indiscriminately – and various CIA funded death squads – which murdered selectively – and the CIA's rampaging palace guard – the 5,000 man strong Iraq Special Operations Forces – the Commandos were part of a genocidal campaign that killed about 10% of the Sunni Arabs of Iraq by 2008, and drove about half of all Sunnis from their homes.

The illegal invasions of Iraq and Libya were sold to us through lies and deceptions. And yet we seemingly remain immune to reasonable, well-documented information that the war on Syria is also being perpetrated by means of lies and deception.

Strategies of deception are being perpetrated by warmongering imperialists in all of these wars, yet despite the ongoing holocaust, and the real threat of nuclear war, the same genocidal strategies are being successfully employed again and again. The public remains oblivious.

What are these strategies, and how can we counter them?

The "soft power complex" engineers domestic hatred towards perennially re-branded enemies, and consent for permanent, illegal warfare, beneath false banners of "democracy," "freedom," or "humanitarian intervention." It also engineers murderous chaos and destabilization in target countries. Sometimes there are unforeseen consequences, but none of the strategies are mistakes, as apologists would have us believe.

Mainstream media often uses public-relations-engineered sources for its stories – the "White Helmets" and the Syrian Observatory for Human Rights (SOHR) are good examples. They often tell their stories using commentators who have largely undisclosed links to the military–industrial complex. An October 2013 analysis by the Public Accountability Initiative discloses widespread conflicts of interest involving twenty-two media commentators who offered ostensibly "objective" commentaries about a previously planned, illegal (future) invasion.[71]

> Additionally, staged theatrical presentations, featuring crisis actors, and purporting to be "reality", are now, arguably, legal. According to an amendment to the 2013 National Defense Authorization Act, House Bill HR 5736, Smith-Mundt Modernization Act (now law), the federal government of the United States can now legally propagandize the domestic public.

---

71. "Conflicts of interest in the Syria debate: An analysis of the defence industry ties of experts and think tanks who commented on military intervention." Public Accountability Initiative. 11 October 2013. Page 6. (http://public-accountability.org/2013/10/conflicts-of-interest-in-the-syria-debate/) Accessed 10 December 2016.

Consequently, not only are we contending with false media source information, corporate media gatekeepers, and commentators with largely undisclosed conflicts of interest, but now we must also contend with fabricated dramas orchestrated to invoke primordial fears and unthinking reactions in mass populations. It is a closed loop circuit of lies, deceptions, and behaviour modification. Recent evidence demonstrates, moreover, that the matrix of deception works brilliantly to engineer consent for the most heinous crimes imaginable.

Democracy demands an informed population, yet governing agencies are working overtime to ensure that their audiences remains deluded. The degenerate controllers are winning. The dystopian future envisioned by Orwell has arrived.

——— CHAPTER VI ———
Syrians Support Their Homeland

B efore the pre-planned Western dirty war on Syria, Syrians respected each other's religions as a personal matter of the soul. Politics and religion were separated by a healthy firewall. Syrians are very well educated: before the war, the levels of illiteracy were very low.

For the most part, Syrians can see through the lies and manipulations of imperial powers that seek to use religion as a wedge issue between groups. They've seen this "divide and conquer" strategy play out in all of the countries that have recently been destroyed, especially in Iraq, and they remember.

When imperialists use this strategy, Syrians are generally immune. They understand that Syria needs to remain pluralist and secular. They understand the imperative of tolerance and they have no need for hate.

Grand Mufti with author Mark Taliano

Syrians understand that they are protecting their homeland from those who seek to impose the extremist, un-Islamic ideology of Wahhabism on the region. Dr Saadeh explains:[72]

> What happened in Ma'loula, it's not revolution. Groups of terrorists attacked the culture and destroyed the culture and destroyed everything good and everything belonging to history, and they want to make us like them and they will kill us because they have the ideology of the Wahhabi and they don't accept another. Either you will be like them or they will kill you. This is the essential ideology for what is called the revolution. And they destroyed Syria by destroying everything in Syria like factories, like anything working to build the culture. And they're supported by America and the European governments.

Slogans about democracy are empty and insulting. When an American tourist questioned an elderly Syrian about democracy, the Syrian exploded with justifiable indignation. Terrorists murdered some of his loved ones – an all-too-familiar tragedy amongst Syrians – and he understands that Obama and his allies are responsible for the foreign-funded terrorism, and that they are equally responsible for the generally unsuccessful efforts to politicize religion in Syria. It has nothing to do with "democracy."

"I support my homeland,"[73] asserted the visibly upset man.

He sees through the lies and confusion to the blunt truth that his homeland needs to be defended from ignorance.

None of the terror groups has the right to impose its barbarous ideology on Syria, and any efforts to do so reflect imperial ambitions to divide and conquer Syria.

When groups such as ISIS–Daesh slaughter people of all faiths in the name of Wahhabi ideology, they are being un-Islamic and they are instruments of anti-religious imperialism.

Likewise, those who make weapons of war for profit are anti-religious. Neither Islam, nor Christianity, nor Judaism, nor any other

---

72. "Dr Joseph Saadeh of Maaloula on Syrian 'revolution." YouTube. 19 September 2016 by Jamal Daoud. Partial transcript. (https://www.youtube.com/watch?v=9oW-bLZCxCZE) Accessed 8 December 2016.
73. The testimony of the Ma'loula man was translated by a guide who accompanied our group through Syria from 16–21 September 2016.

religion supports war for profit. Syria's Grand Mufti teaches this lesson well. Another lesson from the Grand Mufti:

> When politicians use religion as part of their slogans, they are being anti-religious. There must be a clear separation between church and state. Any state that defies humanity by supporting one religion exclusively is a dangerous state.

Syrians and the Syrian Arab Army

Syrians support the Syrian Arab Army. Numerous military check points that slow down traffic are welcomed by Syrians, who often have a friendly and appreciative rapport with the soldiers who are protecting their lives. At one checkpoint, the driver offered a cigar to a soldier and they hugged affectionately. Laughter and collegiality is the rule rather than the exception.

Ali Salem, a Captain in the Syrian Arab Army, also sees through the lies. Ali, like many Syrians and many Syrian soldiers, is well educated. He has a PhD and he is a veterinarian, but when the war broke out his compulsory military service of about 18 months was extended. He explained in Arabic, French, and English that imperial agencies exploited and augmented "Arab Spring" protests by shooting police and military personnel, with a view to creating mayhem and to initiating a war featuring un-Islamic, foreign-funded terrorists. Salem explained that terrorists include Syrian street people, thieves, and criminals; diesel fuel smugglers and drug smugglers; and those who were forced to fight under the threat of death or the death of family members; but terrorists also include "imports" from about eighty foreign countries.

Salem thinks that after the war, schools will have to teach the truth about the war so that the current "crisis" will not repeat itself.

Captain Ali Salem's testimony is corroborated by the testimony of Terrorist Mohammad Faraj Hallaq as recounted by the Syrian Arab News Agency news story "Terrorists in Aleppo's eastern neighborhoods monopolizing food and preventing civilians from leaving."[74] According to Hallaq, the terrorists hoard food, distribute food

---

74. Hazem Sabbagh. "Terrorists in Aleppo's eastern neighborhoods monopolizing food and preventing civilians from leaving." Syrian Arab News Agency. 27 November 2016. (http://sana.sy/en/?p=94445) Accessed 8 December 2016.

only to those who work with the terrorists and obey their orders, force others to fight the Syrian Arab Army (SAA) under the threat of death, imprison protestors, and plant explosions in "humanitarian corridors" to prevent people from escaping terrorist-occupied areas.

The captivity and forced servitude of residents in terrorist-occupied areas is further illustrated by a Facebook post Lilly Martin shared with friends:[75]

> Breaking news from East Aleppo: Oct 21,2016: a family were able to get out to safety! Yes, I watched the interview with them on local TV. The wife said they got tired of waiting so many days to evacuate to safety. They knew that snipers were shooting at people trying to leave, but decided they would take their chances, because he husband was ill and needed medicine and food. They noticed a group of likewise civilians waiting to make a dash for it. They all started running. During their sprint out, 10 civilians with her were shot dead, including a pregnant woman! Her husband said he had been 85 kilos weight, but was now 65 kilos. He was haggard and ill looking, and using one walking cane. The children also stated that they lived in fear of the terrorists. They would not allow children to attend school, they would shoot kids if they stood in the streets and stared at them. Bread had been 25 lira a packet, and was now 1,000 lira. Unbelievable hardships and suffering. I believe these stories because they were coming right out of the mouths of the people, just minutes after running to safety. If it was a reporter recounting stories, I could doubt it, but you can't doubt their stories. I always said to myself that once the people get out of East Aleppo, you will hear horror stories, and these stories will directly reflect on these American backed and supported terrorists. You will also hear the TRUE story later of the White Helmets, it will all be revealed.

Naji Wahbi, another proud Syrian, is mayor of the ancient town of Ma'loula. Terrorists destroyed and looted the ancient shrine of Saint Takla before the Syrian Arab Army defeated them in a bloody battle that cost the lives of 200 Syrian soldiers. Airplanes could not

75. Lilly Martin, Facebook post to friends, 21 October 2016.

assist the Syrians, since the terrorists were armed with modern anti-aircraft weaponry – courtesy of the West and its allies. When asked who is to blame, Wahbi identified Saudi Arabia, Qatar, Turkey, and the USA.[76]

Syria is a holy and brilliant land, steeped in history, still offering newly discovered archaeological treasures to humanity. Syrians, such as those described above, are the valiant defenders on behalf of all of us.

Western Politicians Support Terror

Westerners are critical of the Syrian government, calling it a "regime," calling al-Assad a brutal dictator, and buying the spoon-fed lies, apparently blind to the fact that Western intelligence agencies have totally contaminated their minds to the point where they believe white is black and black is white. Westerners falsely believe that they live in democracies even when there is very little if any difference between the ruling parties; even when the Establishment drives the policies of the preening politicians who have been reduced to the function of public relations agents, and little else.

In Syria, however, the externally-driven war is being resolved internally, and the solutions are often the fruit of a genuine democratic process, in contrast to the fake democratic processes pretending to be democracy in the West.

Dr Ali Haidar, who lost a son to the terrorists, is a member of the official opposition in Syria; not the foreign-backed terrorist "opposition," but the real opposition, and it is from this opposition that the brilliant idea of a "Ministry of Reconciliation" was born, to the chagrin of the Western invaders, and the ultimate approval of the Syrian government.

Whereas the West continues to provide a steady stream of advanced weaponry into the hands of its terrorist proxies, the Ministry of Reconciliation is tasked with removing weapons from terrorist hands. And whereas Western countries support terrorists from ninety-five countries from around the world (about 800 terrorists

---

76. The mayor spoke to our group, The Third International Tour of Peace to Syria. In mid-September 2016.

from Lebanon and Libya, armed with Western weapons, occupied the Krak des Chevaliers, for instance), the Ministry of Reconciliation is tasked with sending them home, unarmed.

The number of foreign-based terrorists in Syria is considerable. Journalist Steven Sahiounie reports that the Turkish President Erdogan:[77]

> used his own mercenary Army of Chinese citizens: the Uygurs. He had allowed them Turkish passports, which they used to pass legally through Central Asia to arrive in Turkey. The immigration officials at the airport in Turkey recognized these special passports, and would confiscate them, but allow the Chinese to pass through legally and enter Turkey. Pres. Erdogan had arranged for them to be transported from the airport in Turkey into Syria through the large and porous border area North of Idlib, which was once a mid-size town in North-West Syria. In the Zeytinburnu distict of Istanbul, Nurali T., a Uyghur Turk working to transport terrorists into Syria, with implicit allowance of the Turkish government, and especially the Turkish Intelligence Services, provides militants with passports worldwide. According to Nurali T.'s office manager, *'More than 50,000 Uyghur Turks came to Turkey with these fake passports from China via Thailand and Malaysia and entered Syria after staying a day in Istanbul.'*

Al-Shamiya Front terrorist flag, East Aleppo

77. Steven Sahiounie. "Erdogan's Al Qaeda Mercenary Army of Uyyghur Chinese 'Jihadists'Dispatched to Syria," *Global Research*, 6 November 2016. (http://www.globalresearch.ca/erdogans-al-qaeda-mercenary-army-of-uyyghur-chinese-jihadists-dispatched-to-syria/5555297) Accessed 5 December 2016.

But there are also Syrian-born terrorists, as mentioned earlier, and those Syrian terrorists who lay down their arms and engage in the "reconciliation" process ultimately either return to their previous civilian jobs (the government will help them with employment and income), or they join brigades of the Syrian Arab Army and fight the real enemy. If they die fighting the real enemy, they become "martyrs" and are somewhat redeemed.

Despite a "Fatwah Declaration" announcing that those who reconcile would be killed, 20,000 Syrian terrorists have so far entered the program and accepted amnesty.[78]

So, whereas the catastrophic dirty war was generated and is sustained from the outside, the solutions to the violence are generated from within and always will be. Any "solutions" offered by the West are necessarily false solutions, since the Western objectives of regime change and/or balkanization of the country would destroy Syria, as happened in Iraq, Libya, Afghanistan, and Ukraine. And the stooge replacement for President al-Assad would be taken from the cesspool of Wahhabi extremists waiting on the sidelines.

Mainstream Media is Corrupt to the Core

The US government enjoys tremendous leeway to basically make things up, especially now that it operates beneath the protective umbrella of the *National Defense Authorization Act*. Yet this has not encouraged reporters to vet sources or to double-source. Certainly it is not happening enough to warrant any reasonable person to think that mainstream media news stories are accurate.

This is no trifling matter. Under international law, much of what passes as "news" in the West is prohibited. It is dangerous and it continues to engineer popular consent for what is essentially an ongoing holocaust in the Middle East.

Reporters should be vetting non-governmental organizations rather than blindly accepting the messaging and amplifying it throughout the world. Writer Vanessa Beeley, who is a member of the Steering Committee at Syria Solidarity Movement International,

---

78. Dr Ali Heidar, Minister for National Reconciliation. The Third International Tour of Peace to Syria visited him at work on 21 September 2016.

reports that these NGOs form a "soft power complex" that serves to advance imperial hegemony (rather than peace and prosperity).[79]

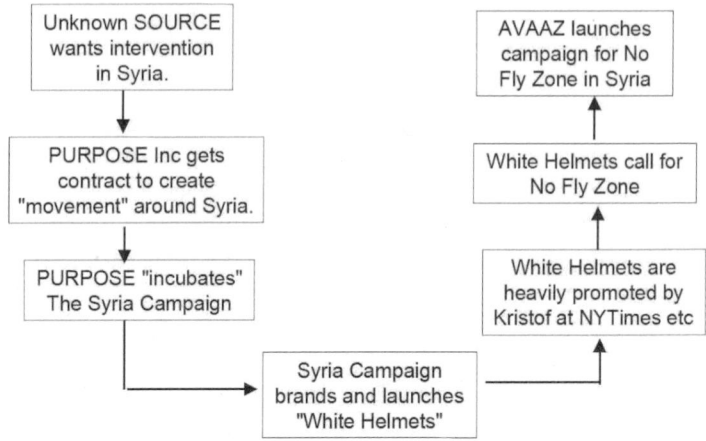

Rick Sterling, for example, shows the sequence of events leading to Avaaz's call for a No Fly Zone in Syria in "Seven Steps of Highly Effective Manipulators":[80]

A compilation of these questionable organizations and individuals, including some that were mentioned earlier, is provided by Eva Bartlett.[81]

Funding sources need to be investigated by those interested in reporting the truth.

79. Patrick Henningsen, The Wall Will Fall. It demonstrates the integration of private "Public Relations"/propaganda companies, (Purpose Inc.) funded by governments and foundations, infiltrated by intelligence operatives, that create fake NGOs (White Helmets), which provide fake source information to important media outlets (NY Times), and promote imperial agendas (No Fly Zone) through partisan social media constructs such as AVAAZ.

80. Rick Sterling. "Seven Steps of Highly Effective Manipulators: White Helmets, Avaaz, Nicholas Kristof and Syria No Fly Zone." Dissident Voice: A Radical Newsletter in the Struggle for Peace and Social Justice. 9 April 2015. (http://dissidentvoice.org/2015/04/seven-steps-of-highly-effective-manipulators/) Accessed 8 December 2016.

81. Eva Bartlett. "'Human Rights' front groups ('Humanitarian Interventionalists') warring on Syria" In Gaza Blog. Not dated. (https://ingaza.wordpress.com/syria/human-rights-front-groups-humanitarian-interventionalists-warring-on-syria/) Accessed 5 December 2016.

We know, for example, that the US Congress funds US Aid and its off-shoots, including the National Endowment for Democracy (NED) and the International Republican Institute (IRI). In a 2014 article entitled "National Endowment of Empire," I explained that:[82]

> Funding flows from the congressional budget of USAID, to NED and its subsidiaries, and finally to factions within target countries whose political economies do not align with globalized economic models of monopoly capitalism.
>
> Beneath NED's democratic veneer is a Board Of Directors replete with members who also represent Fortune 500 companies. Additionally, board members include signatories to the pro-war, pro-corporatocracy Project for a New American Century think tank: Francis Fukuyama, Zalmay Khalizad, Will Marshall, and Vin Weber.

These organizations are fronts for the CIA and serve to effect regime changes throughout the world. They are not "non-governmental." More accurately, they represent illegal foreign interventions in the domestic affairs of "host" countries, all with a view to subordinate other nations to US national interests. Canada is not exempt from illegal foreign interventions in its domestic policies, either. Harper's Conservatives were subservient to US interests.[83]

> In addition to the campaign schools, IRI will be bringing in consultants who specialize in party renovation to discuss case studies of political parties in Germany, Spain, and Canada which successfully carried out the process.

The 'party renovation' referenced in the cable is the 'renovation' of Canada's Progressive Conservative Party into a Republican-inspired Conservative Party of Canada (CPC) that is largely subservient to the U.S Empire south of the border.

---

82. Mark Taliano. "National Endowment of Empire." Whatsupic. 20 October 2014. (http://whatsupic.com/special-usa/national-endowment5344.html) Accessed 8 December 2016.

83. Unclassified cable, Canonical ID 05CARACAS1049_a, "NDI and IRI Work to Strengthen Political Parties in Venezuela" WikiLeaks. 11 April 2005 (https://wikileaks.org/plusd/cables/05CARACAS1049_a.html) accessed 10 December 2016.

Whenever a government has been "renovated" or there is a revolution which devolves into open warfare, these "NGOs" are in the shadows orchestrating the chaos. US AID, as an example, provides funding for the discredited White Helmets (Syria Civil Defense).

In a Facebook post, Janice Kortkamp writes:[84]

> Students at Aleppo University released this video showing their support for the Syrian Army. The university has been the target of brutal bombings by the "rebel" terrorists in Aleppo.
>
> In US main stream media, all you hear about are the attacks on the "rebels" in East Aleppo by the Syrian and Russian forces. And yes, the attacks are tough ... they are trying to rout the terrorist gangs mentioned in this video that have made life in Aleppo hell for several years.
>
> The men and women in the Syrian Army are from every religious and people group in the country. They are fighting an enemy - whether the west calls them "moderates" or not - that is not just brutal, that has not just called for the genocide of many, but an enemy that would make demons proud of their beheadings, tortures, murders, rapes, kidnappings and looting.
>
> I met many soldiers of the army on my trips to Syria and they are my heroes. Their lives are so hard. Some families have sacrificed all their sons in this terrible war.
>
> But it is the "rebels" – the terrorists – who have been car bombing, suicide bombing, and using mortars and exploding bullets on civilian areas, hospitals, schools. A recent attack of theirs on an elementary school cost many children and teachers their lives.
>
> And the "White Helmets" ??? Don't talk to me about the White Helmets!! They are terrorists who have been filmed participating in battles and executions – they make fake propaganda videos for gullible western audiences.

As for the purported "neutrality" of the group, Human Rights Watch argues for bombing in Syria on "humanitarian grounds".[85]

---

84. Janice Kortkamp, Facebook post shared globally, 11 November 2016. Link to video at https://www.youtube.com/watch?v=4ic4p13TD2A&feature=youtu.be
85. Tim Anderson. Facebook photo album "Humanitarian Imperialism," 29 May 2014. (https://scontent-yyz1-1.xx.fbcdn.net/v/t1.0-9/10363933_10203171855230171_6725798032279174834_n.jpg?oh=813de0c1a1950f211f2a9a4c357051e3&oe=58F04769) Accessed 8 December 2016.

Private intelligence agencies are also part of the Soft Power Complex. The Search for International Terrorist Entities Intelligence Group (SITE), for example, provided ISIS beheading videos and pictures. (presumably with a view to engineering public consent for an illegal invasion of Syria under the pretext of fighting ISIS)

News agencies are using SITE as a sole source for news articles, despite the professional obligation to double-source. Author/journalist Naomi Wolf explains on her Facebook page:[86]

> That Google search of how every single major news source is citing SITE with no second source for all their major assertions about the nature of this threat, who did it, what is next ... is so deeply disturbing to me. Fellow journalists: I am not even asking for you to find some other independent source for counterterrorism insights, though that is your job. I am not even asking you to go that far though as you know that – a second source – is de minimis for what should be considered confirmed in our profession. JUST POST THE TWEET. POST THE URL.
>
> SITE claims to find these twitter streams from ISIS ... these extremist websites ... these videos .... online ... there is ONE internet. We should be able to check these destinations online for ourselves with no trouble at all. New York Times, Time Magazine, Guardian, Daily News, Sunday Times, Observer, Wall Street Journal etc etc etc – when your assert that SITE asserts that there are tweets or websites that say x or y – do what is journalistically appropriate. JUST POST THE TWEET OR THE URL SO READERS CAN CHECK FOR THEMSELVES. And if the tweet or url is in Arabic, big deal – it is not cuneiform. There is Google Translate and everyone has friends online in this small connected world who speak Arabic. We can translate them for ourselves. Have YOU, news outlets, even checked the tweets or urls independently? If so why not embed the sources in the digital versions of your articles? Team Humanity can you please reach out to news outlets public editors and ask them to start following this standard journalistic practice?

---

86. Naomi Wolf post, shared globally on Facebook, 15 November 2015. (https://www.facebook.com/naomi.wolf.author/posts/10153717035114476) Accessed 11 December 2016.

A video[87] emerged in October 2015 that illustrates the danger inherent in basing policies and perceptions on discredited sources. A US State Department spokesperson made the very serious allegation that Russia bombed hospitals in Syria. When questioned about the basis for his allegation, the spokesperson referenced press reports, civil society groups, and "operational information." Strong evidence demonstrates, however, that the information is false.

In a recent exchange, the U.S State Department again made unsubstantiated allegations about Russia bombing hospitals. Spokesperson John Kirby failed to identify the locations of the alleged bombings, as well as the Syria relief agencies and "other sources" involved, and he failed to provide a specific list of hospitals allegedly bombed.[88]

In a Facebook posting, independent investigative reporter Vanessa Beeley offered this clarification:[89]

> If you are talking about the government Children's hospital in Aleppo ... it's the only one there ... since 2012 it ceased being a hospital and became Nusra Front HQ and a Sharia Law court, along with the eye hospital.
>
> Perhaps we should clarify the hospitals in Aleppo. Gov't hospitals: Children's and eye hospital. National Hospital was still under construction when the terrorists invaded, so not in use. Then private hospitals: Daqaq, Yassin Jaban, and the Islamic Medical hospital. All those combined only ever had less than 50 beds.
>
> Omar Abdul Aziz hospital set up by the Grand Mufti Badreddin Hassoun. The only two still operational are the Omar Abdul Aziz and Yassin Jaban ... however they are fully occupied by Nusra Front and associated mercenary brigades,

87. "US cites 'press reports' & secret 'operational data' as proof of Russia striking Syrian hospitals" Russia Today. 30 October 2015.
(https://www.rt.com/news/320102-us-blames-russia-syria/) Accessed 8 December 2016.
88. "State Dept dismisses question from RT, says won't treat it like other media." Russia Times. 16 November 2016. (https://www.rt.com/news/367192-kirby-rt-syria-accusations/) Accessed 8 December 2016.
89. Vanessa Beeley, global Facebook post, 20 November 2016. (https://www.face-book.com/vanessa.beeley/posts/10155792071568868) Accessed 5 December 2016.

including Nour Al Din Zinki. Top floors of these two hospitals are used as sniping towers.

No civilians are treated or given priority over terrorist fighters. BBC reported one of the 'last medics in Aleppo' as Dr Osama, 32. Sadly a Facebook post on one of his supporters pages pointed out that on the same date, 8 November, so-called Dr Osama was in Turkey. Fake News.

Syrian resident Lilly Martin offers this further explanation:[90]

When CNN and BBC and MSN talk about 'hospitals being bombed' they are getting reports from the terrorists, who are referring to houses, not hospitals. For example: you live in a neighborhood, and the armed terrorists come in and take over, and they have injured terrorists to treat. They have plenty of the best medicines because that all comes from USA and UK. So, they take over your house and kick you and your family into the street, and presto, your house is now a hospital. Was it ever a hospital before? No. Does anyone on earth know it is a hospital? No, only the local terrorists know that place is a hospital. Then the Syrian or Russian military are bombing terrorists, and their 'hospital' is hit. Was it ever a hospital? No, it was a house in an area infested with terrorists. But, when you watch CNN and BBC it's suddenly a hospital.

These are not trifling lies and misrepresentations, since false intelligence has already served as a catalyst for illegal invasions, and it is likely do so again.

Mainstream media needs to reinvent itself and decide to start reporting evidence-based truth, rather than warmongering propaganda.

---

90. Facebook post by Feroze Mithiborwala,, quoting Janice Kortkamp and shared globally, 21 November 2016.
(https://www.facebook.com/feroze.mithiborwala/posts/10211284020354472) Accessed 12 December 2012.

AFTERWORD

A
t the time of this writing, I am reminded of the terrible irony that the Canadian government supports terrorists in Syria who slaughter and behead Christians.

I am reminded of the terrible toll that Syrians are paying for their freedom – and ours. Facebook friend Hassan Omran just announced that his cousin Baraa was martyred: "To god's heaven the last but not least martyr who defended his land with his soul and blood, my cousin Baraa" (29 November 2016, Facebook post).

But I am also reminded of my first impressions upon visiting Syria. When I awoke on the first morning of my visit, and sat at a table on the polished marble floor beside the fountain, it was still and quiet.

The walls of the hotel courtyard surrounded me — rows of hard, dark basalt stone block and intricately carved soft brown stone were woven together with alcoves and archways, all radiating ancient artistry. High vaulted windows overlooked the courtyard, with plants flowing from balconies and the railings of the narrow corridors leading to rooms.

vanessa beeley @VanessaBeeley · 2h
#Aleppo tonight. Celebrations continue while corporate media sulks. @ReideriArts @Navsteva @21WIRE @theLemniscat @s_ghoshroy

Above was the pale blue cloudless morning sky.

A pigeon lumbered in and perched inside, sheltered by the ancient walls. A native bird, bluish white, swift and silent, swooped in towards the pigeon, and they were both gone, swept away into the Damascene morning.

The quiet returned and the pale blue sky became darker and deeper. Syria will find peace again when this is all over.

Syria is paying, with its blood, for our sins. For this, we should all be grateful.

EPILOGUE

In a classic case of "Reverse Projection" where the West regularly and fraudulently projects its own criminality on the Syrian government, U.S forces are using chemical weapons (weaponized white phosphorous) on Syrian civilians in Raqqa.

Journalist Bill Van Auken describes the impacts of these chemical weapons:

> These incendiary chemical weapons, banned under international law for use in populated areas, ignite human flesh on contact, burning it to the bone, while those who breathe the gases released by the shells suffocate and burn from the inside out. The horrific wounds caused by these weapons reopen when exposed to air. White phosphorus is used to strike terror among those under attack.[91]

U.S. forces are also using MGM – 140B rockets, which detonate in mid-air and scatter about 274 anti-personnel grenades, each of which kills any person within a 15 meter radius.

The anti-personnel/anti-civilian campaigns are driving civilians out of Raqqa, as might be expected.

Beneath the cover of "attacking ISIS", a familiar refrain, the endgame is depopulation and ethnic cleansing. Mint Press News reports that:

> These bombings and the coalition use of chemical weapons have also forced 160,000 civilians to flee Raqqa. Thus, in just one week, Raqqa lost the vast majority of its population, which prior to the conflict in Syria stood at around 220,000.[92]

---

91. Bill Van Auken, "Washington's War Crimes in Syria." Global Research. 16 June, 2017. (http://www.globalresearch.ca/washingtons-war-crimes-in-syria/5594911).
92. Mint Press News, "U.S. Coalition Cleansing Raqqa of Arabs to Expand Kurdish 'Autonomous Region'. June 20, 2017. (http://www.globalresearch.ca/u-s-coalition-cleansing-raqqa-of-arabs-to-expand-kurdish-autonomous-region/5595558#sthash.1cXJW2w3.dpuf), Accessed June 21, 2017

U.S forces, in alliance with Kurdish and SDF proxy forces– and in collusion with Daesh – seek to create the perception that the Kurds are in a position to create a legitimate "statelet" inside of Syrian sovereign territory. Murdering and "cleansing" civilian populations creates a "vacuum" that is then filled with occupation/terrorist forces. This helps to create the false perception that the invaders are somehow "legitimate", and not a minority.

Depopulation also serves a broader imperial agenda. Julian Assange noted in 2015 that "because of the war especially the middle class leaves, doctors, civil servants, lawyers, engineers – precisely those professional groups that you need to keep a country at all functional."[93]

Author and investigative journalist Andrew Korybko also describes the collusion between imperialists and terror groups that furthers imperial agendas:

> The rapid battlefield "successes" are also due in part to the Kurds cutting a deal with Daesh. This isn't a fringe conspiracy theory either, but a documented fact reported by Sergey Surovikin, the commander of Russia's forces in Syria, who told the media just last week that "According to available reliable information, in early June ISIL terrorists entered into collusion with the command of the Kurdish armed units, which are part of the Democratic Forces Union, left the populated localities of Tadia and al-Hamam located 19 kilometers southwest of Raqqa offering no resistance and headed toward Palmyra."[94]

Van Auken confirms that the Western coalition created an escape route for ISIS fighters to leave Raqqa and to redeploy in the province of Daeir ez-Zor, to fight the SAA there, and that a similar strategy was employed in Mosul, where the coalition channelled ISIS fighters from that city to Syria.[95]

---

93. "Wikileaks: Depopulation of Syria is part of the US strategy." South Front, 29 October, 2015. (https://southfront.org/wikileaks-depopulation-of-syria-is-part-of-the-us-strategy/) Accessed 29 June, 2017.

94. Andrew Korybko,"The Kurds Are Ethnically Cleansing Arabs From Raqqa, And The World Is Silent."

95. Bill Van Auken, "Washington's War Crimes in Syria." The Global Politics. 16 June, 2017. (http://global-politics.eu/2017/06/16/washingtons-war-crimes-syria/) Accessed 26 June, 2017.

The credibility of these reports is strengthened by the confirmed report that on 18 June 2017, coalition forces shot down a Syrian warplane that was engaged in combat missions over Raqqa.[96]

In an earlier article, Korybko explained that, "the long-term plan is to carve a second geopolitical 'Israel' in the heart of the Mideast ..."[97]

Korybko's observations are consistent with Journalist Sharmine Narwani's observations. In an article entitled, "Will America Partition Syria?", Narwani also demonstrates how NATO uses ISIS as "strategic assets" :

> ISIS occupied the areas flanking Syria and Iraq's northern border. The US-led coalition has had a presence in these territories for several years, without impairing ISIS control. At the right time, under U.S. cover, Kurds are moving in to "recapture" them.
>
> Kurds constitute a minority in all these governorates, which is how the presence of ISIS became a valuable U.S./Kurdish strategic asset. ISIS's invasion of these areas is delineating the borders of the new entity and de-populating it—creating an opportunity for Washington to champion the Kurds as the primary "liberating" force within those borders, after which Kurds can claim this territorial bounty.[98]

Words spoken by agencies of Western imperialism amount to war propaganda. The bombs, the chemical weapons, the depleted uranium, the missiles, the terrorism are the truth, which is experienced first-hand by all Syrians. In the past year alone, the US military has directly attacked Syrian government

---

96. "US-led coalition downed Syrian army plane in southern Raqqa - Syrian army statement" 18 June, 2017. RT News(https://www.rt.com/news/392941-us-led-coalition-downed-syrian-plane/) Accessed 18 June, 2017

97. Andrew Korybko, "Is there any Kurdish-Daesh-Saudi connection in Syria and Iran?"Global Village Space, June 14, 2017.(http://www.globalvillagespace.com/kurdish-daesh-saudi-connection-syria-iran/")

98. SharmineNarwani, "Will America Partition Syria?" The American Conservative, May 11, 2017 (http://www.theamericanconservative.com/articles/will-america-partition-syria/"

forces at least four times. They shot down a Syrian warplane over Raqqa, as it was attacking ISIS.[99] They bombed the Shayrat airbase in Homs province, a base that the SAA uses to attack ISIS.[100] Additionally, they attacked SAA troops twice, near Syria's southern border with Jordan and Iraq, as SAA forces were approaching the illegal US base at al-Tanf, and were tightening the noose around terrorists including ISIS.[101] All of these attacks – on the dominant forces actually fighting Daesh/ISIS – demonstrate yet again the utter criminality of US-led coalition operations, and the reality that the West uses mercenary terrorists as proxies. These developments are also consistent with "balkanization" plans and the "Plan For A New Middle East"[102], which emerged publicly in 2006. The "Plan For A New Middle East" if realized, would destroy countries like Syria, and indeed the entire Middle East, with a view to ensuring Western and Israeli supremacy and control. Israel, too, has been a direct supporter of ISIS and al Qaeda for years.[103] It treats terrorists in its hospitals for free – even as the same terrorists destroy Syria's hospitals – it provides money and weapons to terrorists, and it has repeatedly bombed targets inside of Syria. A June 2017 report confirms that Israeli forces destroyed SAA tanks, killing Syrian soldiers, in coordination with, and for the benefit of, al Qaeda forces that were

---

99. Paul Craig Roberts, "Another Step toward Devastating War." 19 June, 2017. Paul Craig Roberts Institute For Political Economy.
(http://www.paulcraigroberts.org/2017/06/19/another-step-toward-devastating-war/) Accessed 23 June, 2017

100. Mark Taliano, "The West and Its Allies Seek to Install the 'Black Flag of Terrorism' Over Syria." 10 April, 2017. Global
Research.(http://www.globalresearch.ca/the-west-and-its-allies-seek-to-install-the-black-flag-of-terrorism-over-syria/5584298) Accessed 23 June, 2017.

101. ArabiSouri, "SAA After Outmaneuvering US Forces at al-Tanf Vows Complete Cleaning of Syria from Terrorists."
11 June, 2017. Syria News. (http://www.syrianews.cc/saa-reaches-iraq-borders-northeast-tanf/), Accessed 23 June, 2017

102. Mahdi Darius Nazemroaya, "Plans for Redrawing the Middle East: The Project for a 'New Middle East'" Global Research, 18 November 2006 (http://www.globalresearch.ca/plans-for-redrawing-the-middle-east-the-project-for-a-new-middle-east/3882)

103. WashingtonsBlog, "Turkey and Israel Are Directly Supporting ISIS and Al Qaeda Terrorists In Syria." September 29, 2014
(http://www.washingtonsblog.com/2014/09/turkey-israel-directly-supporting-isis-al-qaeda-syria.html), Accessed June 21, 2017.

attacking Syrian forces in Madinat al-Baath.[104]

The OdedYinon[105] plan, and the notion of a "Greater Israel", foundational documents that underpin Israel's Middle East balkanization strategies, are consistent with the US-led coalition's plans to balkanize and destroy Syria.

It is a criminal, megalomaniacal project unlikely to succeed, given the successes of Syria and its allies in destroying Western terrorist proxy forces inside of Syria.

The war on Syria is a template for two opposing worldviews. Syria and its allies represent a multi-polar model. They represent the rule of international law, military action as an option of last resort, ideological pluralism, and respect for independent societal models. The West and its allies, on the other hand, seek a unipolar world order. They are indifferent to the rule of international law, and they seek to impose their will through military violence, often using proxies, as in Syria. They seek a single societal model, and the rule of the 1%, increasingly supranational, oligarch class.[106] The West and its allies seek a New World Order of globalized war, poverty, and totalitarian control.

Consequently, the US–led dirty war on Syria, a barbaric assault on a cradle of religion and civilization, continues.

Trump's recent trip to Saudi Arabia, a fountainhead of terrorism, and the decision to sell $350 billion worth of weapons to Saudi Arabia, even as he preaches against terrorism, couldn't possibly be more ironic, since Saudi Arabia is a chief weapons dealer and financier to the terrorists in Syria – all in coordination with US–led NATO.

104. Moon of Alabama, "Israel's Fire Support For Its Al-Qaeda Mercenaries Started Three Years Ago." 24 June, 2017. Ron Paul Institute For Peace And Prosperity. (http://ronpaulinstitute.org/archives/peace-and-prosperity/2017/june/24/israels-fire-support-for-its-al-qaeda-mercenaries-started-three-years-ago/) Accessed 25 June, 2017.
105. Mark Taliano. "Israel wants Syria destroyed as presaged by the OdedYinon plan." American Herald Tribune, 25 September, 2016. (http://ahtribune.com/world/north-africa-south-west-asia/syria-crisis/1219-oded-yinon.html). Accessed 21 June, 2017.
106. Mark Taliano, "Western Hegemony vs Russian Sanity" Russia Insider, January 11, 2016

The US also signed a $12 billion military hardware deal with Qatar[107], another source of extremism, and another important US/NATO ally in the dirty war on Syria.

These decisions indicate that the US will continue to support terrorism and extremist ideologies to advance imperial agendas. It is also very telling that the US Congress rejected Tulsi Gabbard's 2017 Stop Arming Terrorists Act.[108]

The West intentionally strengthens the cult of Wahhabism, present in Saudi Arabia and Qatar, since it is this dogma, strict and intolerant, that creates fanatical proxy terrorists: Empire's foot soldiers. Conveniently, Wahhabism also lends itself to Islamophobia, which is then instrumentalized so that Western populations seek war and police state "protections" – oblivious to the fact that their own governments support these terror groups – including al Qaeda and ISIS-Daesh.

It isn't difficult to find evidence that the weapons flow directly to terrorists. NATO weapons caches were found in liberated Aleppo, and more recently, the ISIL weapons caches found in Mosul, Iraq[109] were of Saudi Arabian origin. Additionally, a now-declassified DoD audit reveals that the US army failed to keep track of $1 billion worth of military hardware in Iraq and Kuwait.

Even Amnesty International,[110] which has long-since discredited

---

107. Gareth Jennings, "Qatar agrees purchase of F-15QA fighters from US" IHS Jane's Defence Weekly, 15 June 2017 (http://www.janes.com/article/71443/qatar-agrees-purchase-of-f-15qa-fighters-from-us) Accessed 18 June 2017

108. Washington's Blog, "Why Congress Won't Agree to Stop Arming Terrorists." Global Research, 29 June, 2017. (http://www.globalresearch.ca/why-congress-wont-agree-to-stop-arming-terrorists/5596636) Accessed 29 June, 2017.

109. See LeithFadel, "ISIL weapons from Saudi Arabia seized by Iraqi forces in Mosul: video." Al Masdar News. 20 May 2017 (https://www.almasdarnews.com/article/isil-weapons-saudi-arabia-seized-iraqi-forces-mosul-video/) Accessed 11 June 2016.

110. Amnesty International has been widely criticized by publications that have fact-checked the organization's fraudulent statements and documents about Syria. See, for example, Moon of Alabama's deconstruction of Amnesty International's widely-disseminated report on the Saydnaya Military Prison. (http://www.moonofalabama.org/2017/02/amnesty-report-hearsay.html) This critique is mirrored by Margaret Kimberly in Black Agenda Report (https://www.blackagendareport.com/shamnest-international-human-slaughterhouse).

itself on Syria,[111] and generally serves to advance imperial interests there, admits that: "it makes for especially sobering reading given the long history of leakage of US arms to multiple armed groups committing atrocities in Iraq, including the armed group calling itself the Islamic State."[112]

Naturally, the US would deny that the armaments were intentionally delivered to ISIS and other terrorist groups, but this explanation lacks credibility since there already exists plenty of primary source evidence that the West arms the terrorists.

All of this is consistent with the amended Operation Timber Sycamore,[113] which states unequivocally that the US is tasked with training and providing lethal assistance to terrorists while Saudi Arabia provides money and weapons.

Again, the West's on-going support for terrorists in Syria was in plain view when the US and Canada refused to designate a newly-branded al Qaeda-affiliated group, Hay'at Tahrir al-Sham (HTS), as a terrorist group.

In Canada, a May 2017, CBC report, entitled "Syria's al-Qaeda affiliate escapes from Canada's terror list"[114] notes that:

> The reasons for the reluctance to list the new al-Qaeda formation may have to do with one of its new members, the Noured-Dine Zenki Brigade, a jihadi group from the Aleppo governorate.
>
> The Zenki Brigade was an early and prominent recipient of U.S. aid, weapons and training.

111. Tony Cartalucci, "Amnesty International is U.S State Propaganda." Global Research. 22 August 2012. (http://www.globalresearch.ca/amnesty-international-is-us-state-department-propaganda/32444) Accessed 12 June 2017.
112. "Iraq: US military admits failures to monitor over $1 billion worth of arms transfers." Amnesty International. 27 May 2017.
(https://www.amnesty.org/en/latest/news/2017/05/us-military-admits-failures-to-monitor-over-1-billion-worth-of-arms-transfers/) Accessed 13 June 2017.
113. Martin Berger, "Operation Timber Sycamore And Washington's Secret War on Syria." Mint Press News. 1 December 2016. (http://www.mintpressnews.com/operation-timber-sycamore-washingtons-secret-war-syria/222692/) Accessed 12 June 2017.
114. Evan Dyer, "Syria's al-Qaeda affiliate escapes from Canada's terror list." CBC News. 15 May 2017. (http://www.cbc.ca/beta/news/canada/terror-list-omission-1.4114621) Accessed 11 June 2017.

Zenki was cut off by the State Department only after Amnesty International implicated them in killings of Orthodox Christian priests and members posted a video of themselves beheading a young boy.

In other words, if the West were to acknowledge that HTS (al Qaeda) is a terrorist group, then the Western war criminals would be admitting to their own complicity. And NATO, like the CIA, tries to conceal its criminality beneath the cover of "plausible deniability" whenever possible.

So, the deadly game of providing cover for the terrorists by perennially rebranding them, remains alive.

NATO support for ISIS also remains alive, despite the smoke screens.

Probably the most compelling evidence that proves beyond any reasonable doubt that the West and its allies support ALL of the terrorists in Syria is provided by on-the-ground observers who have visited liberated areas.

French investigative journalist **Pierre Le Corf**'s videos of liberated Sakhour, Aleppo, speak volumes.

Le Corf demonstrates yet again that the White Helmets,[115] important sources for MSM news stories, are al Qaeda affiliates.

In a video recorded at Sakhour, Aleppo, Le Corf takes us for a tour of former al Qaeda and White Helmets headquarters[116] which demonstrates conclusively their close affiliation. The video also demonstrates the close alliances between Daesh/ISIS, FSA, Ahrar al-Sham. All of these groups, including al Qaeda/Jabhat al-Nusra worked together to terrorize Aleppo's citizens for years.

Australian peace activist **Gail Malone** also visited liberated Aleppo, where she toured a hospital, previously occupied by terrorists, where terrorists hoarded medicines, and committed all manner of atrocities.

---

115. "White Helmets – Hand in hand with Al Qaeda." 20 January 2017. (https://youtu.be/GRd8nNjB-pE) Accessed 12 June 2017.
116. Pierre Le Corf, "White Helmets-al Qaeda in Sakhour, Aleppo."12 March 2017. (https://www.youtube.com/watch?v=n5FW2R5B8xQ&feature=youtu.be) Accessed 12 June 2017.

She writes that:[117]

This building (photo 1) was turned from a modern hospital, servicing the community for free, into a place of death and despair. All under the auspices of MSF. Under international law, what was once a hospital was no longer protected, as it was being used for torture and servicing the local takfiri groups. It had forfeited its hospital status.

This MSF 'hospital' had a women's section, a men's section, a Sharia school for the kiddies and a literal dungeon consisting of hundreds of solitary confinement cells and a Sharia Court. A one-stop, Wahhabi terror shop. We saw plenty of evidence of everyone's favourite Oscar winners; the White Helmets had left behind evidence in their rush to stay with their murdering mates on their way to Idlib, following the money as it were …

Photo 1, courtesy Gail Malone

---

117. Gail Malone, "Aleppo: Where hospitals were turned into Sharia gaols." Off Guardian. 17 May 2017. (https://off-guardian.org/2017/05/17/aleppo-where-hospitals-were-turned-into-sharia-gaols/) Accessed 12 June 2017.

Malone's observations are corroborated by an interview with a former prisoner of a hospital jail[118] who recounts the horrors of terrorist-occupied East Aleppo: the torture, the starvation, the executions, the imprisonment, the Sharia law punishments, and the utterly un-Islamic conduct of the terrorist occupiers.

All of the terrorists[119] destroy and occupy schools and hospitals throughout occupied areas of Syria, and all of the terrorists have shared the same destructive goals since the beginning of the war.

In an interview with Syria-based British journalist **Tom Duggan**, Dr. **Saeed Khorasani,** Deputy Minister of Education in Syria, reports that there were 22,100 schools in 2011, but by 2015, the number was reduced to 15,786. Terrorists destroyed 444 schools and occupied 6,433.[120]

Prof. Tim Anderson reports that:[121]

> The al Qaeda groups' attacks on Syria's health system were far more systematic that any one incident could explain.
>
> In just the first three years of this war, before ISIS came to Syria, the NATO and Gulf monarchy-backed armed groups had systematically attacked more than two thirds of Syria's public hospitals, and had murdered, kidnapped or injured more than 300 health workers.

The entire terrorist infrastructure is strengthened with each and every initiative taken by the West and its extremist allies against the legitimate, elected, secular, socially-oriented Syrian government.

118. Pierre Le Corf. Facebook post shared globally. 9 June 2017. 04:33. (https://www.facebook.com/pierrelecorf/videos/10155633153949925/) Accessed 12 June 2017.
119. Eretz Zen, "US Key Man in Syria Worked Closely with ISIL and Jabhat al-Nusra" 17 August 2014. (https://www.youtube.com/watch?v=piN_MNSis1E) Accessed 12 June 2017.
120. Tom Duggan; Sinan Saeed, "ASP Report Tom Duggan and Sinan Saeed, Education Sun of Syria."19 March 2017. (https://www.youtube.com/watch?v=ruBJWB-nsgtM) Accessed 12 June 2017.
121. Tim Anderson, "The 'Aleppo Hospital' Smokescreen: Covering up Al-Qaeda Massacres in Syria, Once Again." Global Research. 9 May 2016. (http://www.globalresearch.ca/the-aleppo-hospital-smokescreen-covering-up-al-qaeda-massacres-in-syria-once-again/5524250) Accessed 13 June 2017.

Illegal sanctions, described by US Congressman **Dennis Kucinich** at the EuroCSE conference in April, 2017, as "war by other means", also serve to advance terrorist capabilities.

U.S Congressman Dennis Kucinich

A conference participant (who chose to remain anonymous) amplified Kucinich's point by explaining that:[122]

> In the case of Syria, they (sanctions) have compounded the deteriorating context by strengthening economies of plunder and acting as a bonus for groups such as ISIS, among other Islamists. These groups successfully recruit from unemployed youth, many of whom are from destitute families, where the main breadwinner has been killed or injured. The experience of Syria over the past five years is well documented in a series of reports from the United Nations Development Programme and the Syrian Center for Policy Research (SCPR).

---

122. Mark Taliano, "The West and Its Allies Seek to Install the 'Black Flag of Terrorism' Over Syria." Global Research. 10 April 2017. (http://www.globalresearch.ca/the-west-and-its-allies-seek-to-install-the-black-flag-of-terrorism-over-syria/5584298) Accessed 11 June 2017.

Refugee camps, another direct result of the West's illegal war on Syria also provide fertile recruiting grounds for terrorists. The Zataari refugee camp in neighbouring Jordan reportedly serves this function.[123]

Organ harvesting remains one of the terrorists' lucrative and heinous operations to generate money. According to Hossein Noufel, Director-General of the Syrian Coroner's office,

"body organs of thousands of Syrian civilians have been sold in the international black markets over the past six years."[124]

The aforementioned information is corroborated by permanent Syrian resident, **Lilly Martin**, who commented in a global Facebook posting that:[125]

> The organ harvesting in Turkey is not limited to selling a part for cash. The majority of organ harvesting in Turkey is done by the terrorists, who are US supported. The terrorists take injured or kidnapped Syrians across the border to Turkey and instead of saving their life with medical care, the injured are shipped back to Syria with an explanation that they died in surgery, and couldn't be saved. However, they always have clear signs of organ harvesting. In many cases, eyes were re-moved. This info comes from survivors of the Aleppo battles, who are now in Latakia.

The litany of un-Islamic crimes committed by NATO terrorists is seemingly endless. **Ewelina U. Ochab** describes the degeneracy of sex slavery in a March 2, 2017 article, "Sexual Violence As A

123. John Rosenthal, "UNHCR Refugee Camp in Jordan: Safe Haven for Jihadist Rebels and Arms Shipments into Syria." Global Research. 12 November 2013.From Asia Times 8 November 2013. (http://www.globalresearch.ca/unhcr-refugee-camp-in-jordan-safe-haven-for-jihadist-rebels-and-arms-shipments-into-syria/5357816) Accessed 11 June 2017.

124. "Coroner's Office: Body Organs of Over 15,000 Syrians Sold in 6 Years." FARS News Agency. 17 November 2016. (http://en.farsnews.com/newstext.aspx?nn=1395082700037 3) Accessed 11 June 2017.

125. Mark Taliano, "NATO Terrorism in Syria." Global Research. 2 May 2017. (http://www.globalresearch.ca/nato-terrorism-in-syria/5588236) Accessed 11 June 2017.

Weapon Of War: The Story Of Daesh And Boko Haram." She explains that:[126]

> During my recent trip to Iraq, I was shown a document, dated October 16, 2014, listing the prices for the purchase of Yazidi and Christian girls and women. The prices ranged from 75,000 Iraqi Dinar (about $64) for a thirty- to forty-year-old woman, to 200,000 Iraqi Dinar (about $170) for a girl between one and nine years old. Overall, the younger the girl or woman was, the higher the price to be paid – the sight of such prices being paid for babies and young children filled me with unimaginable horror at the pain they would go through.
>
> So, for as little as $64.00-170.00, Yazidi and Christian girls would become the property of Daesh fighters, who would then subject them to abuse on a daily basis …

Reverend **Andrew Ashdown**, another on-the-ground observer of war-torn Syria, observed in a global Facebook commentary, dated April 11, 2017, that:

> When I visited an IDP (Internally Displaced Centre) in Latakia last year, everyone had horrific stories of the brutality they had suffered at the hands of our 'moderate' 'rebels'. One of them said: "We don't need the 'freedom' the Jihadists are calling for. We had a good life before. Leave us alone. We've had enough of your 'freedom'." Many others say they've seen the kind of 'Democracy' the Islamist terrorists will bring to their country… in the murder and torture of anyone who disagrees with their ideology. Those are the people whom our western governments are backing…"[127]

These testimonies are consistent with what Henry Lowendorf, a

---

126. Ewelina U. Ochab, "Sexual Violence As A Weapon Of War: The Story Of Daesh And Boko Haram." Forbes. 2 March 2017. (https://www.forbes.com/sites/ewelinaochab/2017/03/02/sexual-violence-as-a-weapon-of-war-the-story-of-daesh-and-boko-haram/2/#1152859b4b97) Accessed 12 June 2017.
127. Comment by Ashdown on his own Facebook post, 11 April 2017. (https://www.facebook.com/andrew.ashdown.9/posts/1860240943993468?comment_id=1860326493984913&comment_tracking=%7B%22tn%22%3A%22R2%22%7D)

member of the Executive Board[128] of the US Peace Council's Peace and Fact-Finding Delegation to Syria, reported in August, 2016:

> What we saw (in Syria) goes against everything we read in the United States ... When you go to Syria, which I did last month, the popularity of the government and the Syrian Arab Army is rampant. It's not out of some dream fantasy. It comes obviously from the government and the army being the only thing between living a secular life on the one hand and the hatred and violence of ISIS and the various other terrorist groups underwritten by the terrorist Saudis and US and their allies on the other. The refugees who don't leave Syria do not flee to the terrorist side, they flee to the government side, in huge numbers. So would all of us in similar circumstances ...[129]

All of the chaos, the refugees, the terrorist proxies, the mass murder, is engineered by the West and its allies. Washington neo-cons have even given it a benign-sounding label, "Creative Chaos".[130]

The reality is an inversion of the propaganda lies fed to Western audiences. In fact, President Assad must stay, for the sake of civilization, and for the sake of destroying Western-backed terrorism. Each time Empire succeeds in destroying another country, the problem of terrorism worsens – as might be expected.

Needless to say, there is a huge disconnect between what is really happening in Syria, based on factual, primary source, fully-corroborated evidence, versus the fictional warmongering narratives provided to Western audiences.

For example, the alleged sarin gas attack at Khan Sheikhoun,[131]

128. "U.S. Peace Council's Peace and Fact-Finding Delegation Returns from Syria." 11 August 2015. (http://iacenter.org/2514/u-s-peace-councils-peace-and-fact-finding-delegation-returns-from-syria/) Accessed 13 June 2017.
129. Mark Taliano. "Henry Lowendorf: What we saw in Syria goes against everything we read in the United States." American Herald Tribune. 15 August 2016. (http://ahtribune.com/opinion/1148-henry-lowendorf.html). Accessed 11 June 2017.
130. Mark Taliano, "'Creative Chaos' and the War Against Humanity. US-NATO Supports ISIS." Global Research. 29 May 2017. (http://www.globalresearch.ca/creative-chaos-and-the-war-against-humanity-us-nato-supports-isis/5592499) Accessed 11 June 2017.
131. Ted Postol."Important Correction: The Nerve Agent Attack that did Not Occur, Khan Sheikhoun, Syria." Global Research. 25 April 2017. (http://www.globalresearch.ca/important-correction-the-nerve-agent-attack-that-did-not-occur-khan-sheikhoun-syria/5586891) Accessed 13 June 2017.

Syria, on April 4, 2017, was shown to be false flag terrorism engineered to provide a pretext for an escalation of US/NATO war crimes in Syria.

Professor Emeritus of Science, Technology, and National Security Policy at the Massachusetts Institute of Technology, Theodore Postol, makes these important points:

• The White house document does not provide evidence that the Syrian government was the source of the chemical attack at Khan Sheikhoun.

• Key evidence points to an attack from the ground, and not from the air.

• There is no evidence that the crater was created by sarin munitions dropped from the air.

• The incident is similar to the August 2013 alleged nerve gas attack in Damascus of which President Obama was misinformed that the Syrian government was the perpetrator.

Similarly, the narrative about Omran, "the boy in the orange chair" was also proven fraudulent. Investigative reporter Eva Bartlett interviewed Omran's father, in Syria, and reported on a June 2017, Facebook commentary that the story is built on a "mountain of lies."[132]

Bartlett explains in "MintPress Meets The Father Of Iconic Aleppo Boy, Who Says Media Lied About His Son" that:

> While the entire details of the August 17 2,016 [sic] evening are not yet clear, what is clear is that the White Helmets, the AMC, and the corporate media lied and exploited Omran Daqneesh and his family in their concerted war propaganda efforts to demonize the Syrian and Russian governments.[133]

---

132 Eva Bartlett. Facebook post shared globally. 7 June 2017.00:29.

133. Eva Bartlett, "MintPress Meets The Father Of Iconic Aleppo Boy, Who Says Media Lied About His Son." MintPress News. 9 June 2017.

(http://www.mintpressnews.com/mintpress-meets-father-iconic-aleppo-boy-says-media-lied-son/228722/) Accessed 11 June 2017.

Presumably, if Westerners knew the truth, they would be appalled, and they would not support the lies from elected politicians and from fabricated MSM news stories.

Not only have dark state agencies engineered **consent** for war and terrorism but they have also engineered **dissent**.

Whereas genuine grassroots movements do exist, protests in the West and the globalized world can be heavily influenced by 'establishment' factions. In some cases, corporate and government elites channel popular frustrations by balkanizing movements or by pitting one establishment faction against another. They do so with the intent of neutralizing dissent, and obscuring fundamental issues.

Absent from the January 2017 Women's March[134] on Washington, for example, was any concern for women in Syria who are being threatened by Western-backed terrorists,[135] and who will be forced to live and abide by fundamentalist interpretations of Sharia Law (and currently live under such conditions in terrorist-occupied areas). The U.S. Women's March mobilized demonstrators based on ideas of feminism and concerns about President Trump's domestic policy, but did nothing to address the interventionist policies of permanent war that guide both Democratic and Republican factions in the United States.

Advertised through the mainstream media, and the echo chambers of corporate messaging, the Women's March was instead a colourful act of political theatre, with pink-hatted demonstrators posing for photos with police. The event represented "controlled" opposition.

Likewise, environmentalists are missing the elephant in the room when they fail to denounce war, which is one of the worst polluters.[136]

Those who oppose bio-technology and neoliberal/predatory economic systems are also missing a root cause when they do not protest against criminal warfare, since war advances the tentacles of monopoly capitalism, neoliberalism, and corporate control over humanity.

134. Mark Taliano, "Women's March For Misogyny?" Global Research. 26 January 2017. (http://www.globalresearch.ca/womens-march-for-misogyny/5570900) Accessed 13 June 2017.
135. Mark Taliano, "U.S–Led NATO's Tree Of Lies." Global Research. 17 May 2017. (http://www.globalresearch.ca/u-s-led-natos-tree-of-lies/5590456) Accessed 13 June 2017.
136. Whitney Webb. "U.S. Military Is World's Biggest Polluter." MintPress News. 15 May 2017. (https://www.ecowatch.com/military-largest-polluter-2408760609.html) Accessed 11 June 2017.

Those who oppose mass incarceration and widespread poverty,[137] particularly in the US, would also do well to oppose illegal warfare, since the huge sums of public monies spent on war should be spent for the benefit and uplift of the public, and the broad-based economy.

And, of course, those who protest police state legislation should be opposing criminal warfare since war crushes human rights as a matter of course.

War is anti-human rights, anti-democracy, anti-environment, anti-sustainable economics, and anti-life. Yet, war is conspicuously missing from protest movements. All protest groups (except pro-war groups) should assemble together beneath an anti-war banner. Unity is strength and it is what neo-con warmongers fear the most among their opposition.

Any protest movement which is funded by foundations or fake NGOs is counter-productive. Controlled opposition, mentioned above, balkanizes broad-based protest movements.

Prof. Chossudovsky notes in "Rockefeller, Ford Foundations Behind World Social Forum (WSF). The Corporate Funding of Social Activism"[138] for example, that the 2016 World Social Forum received funding from corporate foundations including Ford, Rockefeller, Tides, et al.

He notes that, "there is an obvious contradiction: another world is not possible when the campaign against neoliberalism is financed by an alliance of corporate donors firmly committed to neoliberalism and the US-NATO military agenda."

Another example of controlled opposition, or the "parallel Left", would be programs such as Democracy Now, which amplify evidence-free (war-mongering) narratives about the war on Syria, even as they exclude evidence-based (peace-making) narratives. Reportedly, Democracy Now chose not to interview Vanessa Beeley, who

---

137. "Study By MIT Economist: U.S. Has Regressed To A Third-World Nation For Most Of Its Citizens." The Intellectualist. 20 April 2017. (https://theintellectualist.co/study-mit-economist-u-s-regressed-third-world-nation-citizens/) Accessed 11 June 2017.
138. Michel Chossudovsky, "Rockefeller, Ford Foundations Behind World Social Forum (WSF). The Corporate Funding of Social Activism." Global Research. 10 August 2016. (http://www.globalresearch.ca/rockefeller-ford-foundations-behind-world-social-forum-wsf-the-corporate-funding-of-social-activism/5540552) Accessed 11 June 2017.

is an expert on the White Helmets, but did interview Anand Gopal,[139] who demonstrates support for the war on Syria. Similarly, at the time of this writing, Democracy Now has failed to report on Seymour Hersh's recent revelations – involving military and intelligence transcripts of real-time communications – that adds to the mountain of primary source evidence which disproves Washington's stories about the alleged sarin gas attack at Khan Sheikhoun, Idlib Province, Syria. Hersh's evidence-based conclusion? "Syria did not drop a sarin bomb that morning. It was known to everybody in the command. Period."[140]

The UN itself, having been marginalized for decades by U.S. hegemony and exceptionalism, now suffers a new embarrassment. Saudi Arabia, an absolute monarchy where political parties and unions are banned, where women are not permitted to drive, and where egregious human rights violations are the norm, has become a member of the UN Human Rights Council.[141] Only the dominance of the US over that body prevents the Saudis from being laughed off stage.

The West's current trajectories of pursuing criminal warfare to satisfy unelected elites through a shadow state – causing death, poverty, and terrorism globally – contradicts everything that is sane and life-enhancing.

Syrians know first-hand what it's like to be victimized by NATO's sectarian, anti-democratic terrorists, by illegal sanctions, and by terror campaigns that target civilians, civilian infrastructure,

---

139. Danny Haiphong, " 'Democracy Now' Runs Interference for Imperialism in Syria." American Herald Tribune. 12 May, 2017.(http://www.globalresearch.ca/democracy-now-runs-interference-for-imperialism-in-syria/5590162) Accessed 24 June, 2017.
140. "People should be tearing into the BBC for the alarming decision it just made." The Canary. 30 June, 2017. (https://www.thecanary.co/2017/06/30/people-tearing-bbc-alarming-decision-just-made-video/) Accessed 02 July, 2017.
141. Michaela Whitton, "Wikileaks Exposes Secret Deal To Get Saudi Arabia On UN Human Rights Council." Mint Press News. 6 October 2015. (http://www.mintpressnews.com/wikileaks-exposes-secret-deal-to-get-saudi-arabia-on-un-human-rights-council/210117/) Accessed 11 June 2017.

and SAA soldiers alike.

A political economy such as ours, that requires vast outlays of public monies to support this life-destroying globalized agenda, is surely a system that is best suited for the dustbin of history.

GLOBAL RESEARCH PUBLISHERS

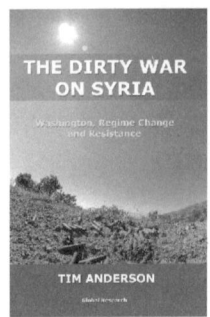

The Dirty War on Syria: Washington, Regime Change and Resistance
TIM ANDERSON
ISBN 978-0-9737147-8-4 (2016), 240 pages

The Dirty War on Syria has relied on a level of mass disinformation not seen in living memory. In seeking 'regime change' the big powers sought to hide their hand, using proxy armies of 'Islamists', demonising the Syrian Government and constantly accusing it of atrocities. In this way Syrian President Bashar al Assad, a mild-mannered eye doctor, became the new evil in the world.

As western peoples we have been particularly deceived by this dirty war, reverting to our worst traditions of intervention, racial prejudice and poor reflection on our own histories. This book tries to tell its story while rescuing some of the better western traditions: the use of reason, ethical principle and the search for independent evidence.

Dr Tim Anderson is a Senior Lecturer in Political Economy at the University of Sydney. He researches and writes on development, rights and self-determination in Latin America, the Asia-Pacific and the Middle East.

The Globalization of War: America's "Long War" against Humanity
MICHEL CHOSSUDOVSKY
ISBN 978-0-9737147-6-0 (2015), 212 pages

America's hegemonic project in the post 9/11 era is the "Globalization of War" whereby the U.S.-NATO military machine —coupled with covert intelligence operations, economic sanctions and the thrust of "regime change"— is deployed in all major regions of the world. The threat of pre-emptive nuclear war is also used to black-mail countries into submission.

This "Long War against Humanity" is carried out at the height of the most serious economic crisis in modern history.

It is intimately related to a process of global financial restructuring, which has resulted in the collapse of national economies and the impoverishment of large sectors of the World population.

The ultimate objective is World conquest under the cloak of "human rights" and "Western democracy".

Award winning author and economics professor Michel Chossudovsky is Director of the Centre for Research on Globalization (CRG).

All titles can be ordered online at https://store.globalresearch.ca/

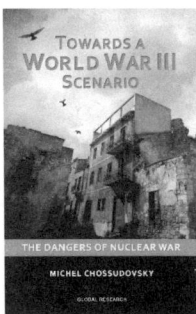

Towards a World War III Scenario: The Dangers of Nuclear War
MICHEL CHOSSUDOVSKY
ISBN 978-0-9737147-5-3 (2012), 102 pages.

The U.S. has embarked on a military adventure, "a long war", which threatens the future of humanity. U.S.-NATO weapons of mass destruction are portrayed as instruments of peace. Mini-nukes are said to be "harmless to the surrounding civilian population". Pre-emptive nuclear war is portrayed as a "humanitarian undertaking".

While one can conceptualize the loss of life and destruction resulting from present-day wars including Iraq and Afghanistan, it is impossible to fully comprehend the devastation which might result from a Third World War, using "new technologies" and advanced weapons, until it occurs and becomes a reality. The international community has endorsed nuclear war in the name of world peace. "Making the world safer" is the justification for launching a military operation which could potentially result in a nuclear holocaust.

The object of this book is to forcefully reverse the tide of war, challenge the war criminals in high office and the powerful corporate lobby groups which support them.

The Global Economic Crisis:
The Great Depression of the XXI Century
MICHEL CHOSSUDOVSKY AND ANDREW GAVIN
MARSHALL, EDITORS
ISBN 978-0973714739 (2010), 416 pages

In all major regions of the world, the economic recession is deep-seated, resulting in mass unemployment, the collapse of state social programs and the impoverishment of millions of people. The meltdown of financial markets was the result of institutionalized fraud and financial manipulation. The economic crisis is accompanied by a worldwide process of militarization, a "war without borders" led by the U.S. and its NATO allies.

This book takes the reader through the corridors of the Federal Reserve, into the plush corporate boardrooms on Wall Street where far-reaching financial transactions are routinely undertaken.

Each of the authors in this timely collection digs beneath the gilded surface to reveal a complex web of deceit and media distortion which serves to conceal the workings of the global economic system and its devastating impacts on people's lives.

Seeds of Destruction:
The Hidden Agenda of Genetic Manipulation
F. WILLIAM ENGDAHL
ISBN 978-0-937147-2-2 (2007), 341 pages

This skillfully researched book focuses on how a small socio-political American elite seeks to establish control over the very basis of human survival: the provision of our daily bread. *"Control the food and you control the people."*

This is no ordinary book about the perils of GMO. Engdahl takes the reader inside the corridors of power, into the backrooms of the science labs, behind closed doors in the corporate boardrooms.

The author cogently reveals a diabolical world of profit-driven political intrigue and government corruption and coercion, where genetic manipulation and the patenting of life forms are used to gain worldwide control over food production. If the book often reads as a crime story, that should come as no surprise. For that is what it is.

Engdahl's carefully argued critique goes far beyond the familiar controversies surrounding the practice of genetic modification as a scientific technique. The book is an eye-opener, a must-read for all those committed to the causes of social justice and world peace.

F. William Engdahl is a leading analyst of the New World Order and author of the best-selling book on oil and geopolitics, A Century of War: Anglo-American Politics and the New World Order.

America's "War on Terrorism"
MICHEL CHOSSUDOVSKY
ISBN 0-9737147-1-9 (2005), 387 pages

In this 2005 best-selling title, the author blows away the smokescreen put up by the mainstream media that 9/11 was an attack on America by "Islamic terrorists". Through meticulous research, the author uncovers a military-intelligence ploy behind the September 11 attacks, and the cover-up and complicity of key members of the Bush administration.

This expanded edition, which includes twelve new chapters, focuses on the use of 9/11 as a pretext for the invasion and illegal occupation of Iraq, the militarization of justice and law enforcement and the repeal of democracy.

According to Chossudovsky, the "war on terrorism" is a complete fabrication based on the illusion that one man, Osama bin Laden, outwitted the $40 billion-a-year American intelligence apparatus. The "war on terrorism" is a war of conquest. Globalization is the final march to the New World Order, dominated by Wall Street and the U.S. military-industrial complex.

September 11, 2001 provides a justification for waging a war without borders. Washington's agenda consists in extending the frontiers of the American empire to facilitate complete U.S. corporate control, while installing within America the institutions of the Homeland Security State. Chossudovsky peels back layers of rhetoric to reveal a complex web of deceit aimed at luring the American people and the rest of the world into accepting a military solution which threatens the future of humanity.

***The Globalization of Poverty
and the New World Order***
MICHEL CHOSSUDOVSKY
ISBN 09737147-0-0 (2003), 403 pages

In this new and expanded edition of Chossudovsky's international best-seller, the author outlines the contours of a New World Order which feeds on human poverty and the destruction of the environment, generates social apartheid, encourages racism and ethnic strife and undermines the rights of women. The result as his detailed examples from all parts of the world show so convincingly, is a globalization of poverty.

This book is a skillful combination of lucid explanation and cogently argued critique of the fundamental directions in which our world is moving financially and economically.

In this new enlarged edition – which includes ten new chapters and a new introduction – the author reviews the causes and consequences of famine in Sub-Saharan Africa, the dramatic meltdown of financial markets, the demise of state social programs and the devastation resulting from corporate downsizing and trade liberalization.